Psychological
Explanation

A Random House Study in the Problems of Philosophy

STUDIES IN PHILOSOPHY
Consulting Editor:
V. C. CHAPPELL, *The University of Chicago*

Psychological Explanation

An Introduction to the
PHILOSOPHY of PSYCHOLOGY

JERRY A. FODOR

Massachusetts Institute of Technology

RANDOM HOUSE *New York*

PREFACE

I think many philosophers secretly harbor the view that there is something deeply (i.e., conceptually) wrong with psychology, but that a philosopher with a little training in the techniques of linguistic analysis and a free afternoon could straighten it out.

Several years ago I found myself with a free afternoon. This book represents a tentative attempt to put bits of the psychology I have since picked up together with some of my philosophical prejudices. I hope in this way to arrive at a preliminary analysis of the character of some of the theoretical constructs employed in the areas of psychology that have particularly interested me. It goes without saying that much has had to be left unclear, partly because of limitations of space, but largely because the problems are very hard and there is much that I remain unclear about. I have arrived at some views about what theories of psychological explanation won't work, however, and these include a number that are currently fashionable. I also have some views about where the heart of the problem about psychological explanation may lie, and those views will be set forth here.

I want to emphasize that what I have to say concerns a rather special kind of psychological explanation, the kind in which we account for the behavior of an organism by referring to its psychological states. This sort of account is, perhaps, more characteristic of certain branches of learning theory and perception theory than, say, of social or developmental psychology. To the extent that this is the case, my discussion of psychological explanation is likely to be more relevant to theories in the former areas than in the latter. Thus, for example, I shall have nothing at all to say about psychological explanations in which behavior is accounted for by appeal to statistical regularities, to developmental norms, and so on.

I have discussed the issues that are examined in this book with a number of philosophers on a number of occasions. Among them, I am particularly indebted to Professors R. Abelson, D. Armstrong, C. Chihara, H. Feigl, R. Freed, L. Linsky, P. Meehl, J. F. Thomson, F. Will, and P. Ziff for suggesting points that I have found helpful. The errors and unclarities in what follows are, however, not their responsibility, being entirely of my own devising.

Various psychologists have borne with me while I attempted to educate myself in their discipline, some even to the extent of permitting me to use their hard-earned experimental gear. For such charities I am particularly indebted to Professor C. E. Osgood of the Institute for Communications Research, University of Illinois, and Professor H. L. Teuber of the Department of Psychology, M.I.T. I wish also to thank the Research Laboratory of Electronics, M.I.T., for their support of psycholinguistic research, some of which is reported informally in Chapter II, and the Center for Advanced Study in the Behavioral Sciences at Palo Alto, California for the research fellowship during the tenure of which the major portion of the work on the manuscript of this book was completed.

Parts of Chapter I appeared in The Journal of Philosophy, *LXIII (June, 1966) under the title "Could There Be A Theory of Perception?" Permission to use this material here is gratefully acknowledged.*

Finally, I wish to acknowledge two profound intellectual obligations. Readers who are familiar with the work of Professor Noam Chomsky on linguistic theory and metatheory will hardly fail to detect its influence on the general approach to psychological explanation taken here. Indeed, this book is in part an attempt to make explicit some aspects of a view of psychological explanation that comports naturally with the generative approach to language. Equally clear should be my obligation to Professor Hilary Putnam, from whose work on the mind-body problem and on the analysis of scientific theories I have greatly benefited.

J.A.F.

Cambridge, Massachusetts

CONTENTS

INTRODUCTION

Aristotle held that the philosophy of science is required to provide a general characterization of the principles and procedures that the sciences have in common and also to enumerate their methodological peculiarities: "We must say what reasoning is, and what its varieties are . . ." In doing the former, we exhibit the general character of rational inquiry; in doing the latter, we determine the impact that differences in subject matter make upon preferred modes of investigation and explanation. In either case, the goal of the philosopher is to say how the game is played: to describe what counts as good practice in scientific inquiry and argument.

Modern philosophy of science has been largely devoted to the first of the investigations Aristotle distinguishes. Philosophers of science have generally understood their task to be that of providing a reconstruction of the successful practices of working scientists insofar as such practices are common to all fields of scientific inquiry. In consequence, an impressive body of philosophical information has been accumulated and important insights have been achieved with regard to such matters as the nature of confirmation, the logical structure of scientific theories, the formal properties of statements that express laws, the character of theoretical entities, and so on.

The philosophical discussion of the special sciences has, however, often been devoted to more ambitious but less prom-

ising pursuits. Thus, among those philosophers who are interested in the behavioral sciences, some have been primarily concerned with helping to make psychology "scientific" by laying down guidelines for how it can conform to practices that are alleged to characterize the methodology of more advanced disciplines. Others have attempted to show that the very objective of producing theories of behavior is the consequence of wholesale conceptual confusion and ought therefore to be abandoned. Still others have interested themselves in behavioral theories only insofar as such theories can be supposed to cast light upon specifically philosophical problems about minds and bodies. Surprisingly few philosophers have been willing to discuss psychological theories in particular in the way in which most philosophers now discuss scientific theories in general, namely, as the consequence of a form of intellectual enterprise whose character and structure it is the goal of the philosopher to describe.

In consequence, psychological metatheory has remained seriously underdeveloped. With a few important exceptions,[1] its history during the second quarter of this century has been an attempt to work out a variety of behaviorism that would satisfy the constraints imposed on psychological explanation by an acceptance and application of empiricist (and particularly operationalist) views of general scientific method. The better known accounts of psychological explanation have thus often failed to reflect the most important movement in current philosophy of science: the attempt to determine the consequences of rejecting key features of the empiricist program.[2] Verificationism as an account of meaning; conventionalism as an account of theoretical constructs; sharp distinction between the observational and inferential language of theories; uncritical reliance upon the analytic-synthetic distinction—all these have recently come into question among philosophers of science who have realized that these doctrines are by no means indispensable to characterizations of scientific explanation and confirmation and that philosophical accounts that exploit them may in fact seriously distort the realities of scientific practice. Yet it is upon precisely these views that much of the implicit and explicit metatheory of American experimental psychology appears to rest.

That widely accepted accounts of psychological explanation should suffer from this lack of philosophical sophistication is doubly unfortunate since it is precisely in the new sciences that methodological commitments are likely to make the most immediate impact upon actual scientific practice. Lacking both well-entrenched paradigms of successful theory construction and examples of well-tried laboratory procedures, a psychologist is likely to appeal his decisions about research strategies directly to general methodological principles to an extent to which a physicist or chemist does not. The mark of a mature science is the existence of routine problems—that is, the existence of problems that can be identified a priori as likely to succumb to well-known methods of inquiry and modes of explanation. There are few routine problems in psychology; consequently, methodological discussions fill the journals and methodological disagreements translate rather directly into differences in experimental design. A consequence of the unsettled state of psychological metatheory is thus that schools of psychology are distinguished as much by the kinds of experiments that their adherents typically perform as by the theories that they espouse.

For example, it is not surprising that a methodological dispute such as the one between learning theory and Gestalt psychology should have manifested itself in differences between the accounts of perception that the two movements produced. What is striking is how directly the behaviorism of the learning theorist dictated the discrimination experiment as the typical paradigm for his laboratory investigations of perception, for this was a paradigm that the Gestalt theorist employed incidentally, if at all. Roughly, if one is methodologically committed to the behavioristic assumption of an "empty" organism, one must suppose that the perceptual distinctions an organism makes correspond directly to discriminable physical distinctions in its input. If, on the other hand, one's methodological views permit one to suppose that perceptual discriminations may be the consequences of mental operations of some complexity, the expectation that the distinctions an organism can make should turn out to be isomorphic to physical differences between stimuli is rendered correspondingly implausible and the discrimination experiment appears less obviously to be the correct instrument for the experimental investigation of perception. Rather, one is likely to turn, as the Gestalt investigators in fact did, to experimental designs that permit the study of such phenomena as perceptual ambiguity, perceptual illusion, and perceptual bias: phenomena in which the organism's contribution to processes of perceptual organization is directly revealed.

Such examples suggest the importance for psychological practice of providing an explicit and detailed account of psychological explanation. The problems that need to be unraveled in such an undertaking are, however, formidable, and only three strands have been traced in this book. First, the present discussion aims to show that the case for operationalism is no stronger in psychology than it has proved to be in the other sciences. Second, I have tried to survey some of the outstanding philosophical issues that a serious theory of psychological explanation will have to face and, occasionally, to suggest approaches to these problems that seem to me to be worth pursuing. Finally, I argue in Chapters III and IV that the notions of function and of functional equivalence have a central role to play both in characterizations of the goals of *theory construction in psychology and in accounts of the relations between psychology and such neighboring disciplines as neurology.*

It is, indeed, a main purpose of this book to suggest some of the ways in which outstanding issues in the philosophy of psychology tend to converge upon the notion of functional equivalence. Since, however, the term "function" itself designates a moot problem in philosophical discussions of the biological sciences, and since I shall not be concerned to offer a solution to that problem but only to show what aspects it bears in psychology, a few prefatory remarks about the general question of functional analysis might be in place here.

It is a fact that the pupil of the human eye is a diaphragm. Is it in the same sense a fact that the function of the pupil is to regulate incident light? The classic treatments of this sort of question in the philosophy of the biological sciences[3] have been attempts to analyze biological statements of the form "Q is the function of X" in terms of strictly causal statements, presumably of the form "X is an empirically necessary condition for Q." A scheme that provided a uniform way of effecting such translations would ipso facto permit the elimination of functional explanations from the biological sciences, thereby demonstrating that the biologist's occasional employment of such explanations produces no special problems for the philosopher of science.

Attempts to eliminate notions of function in favor of the notion of empirically necessary conditions have, however, not thus far proved successful. This is largely because, as Hempel has pointed out, biological states and structures often have adventitious consequences that may have little or nothing to do with those of their effects that the biologist wishes to identify as their functions. Thus, the presence of chlorophyll is an empirically necessary condition for photosynthesis in

*plants. But that consideration alone does not suffice to dem-
onstrate that the function of chlorophyll is to perform photosynthesis, since having chlorophyll is equally an empirically
necessary condition for a plant to be green. How, then, are
we to defend the conclusion that the function of chlorophyll
is to perform photosynthesis and not to provide coloration?
Analogously, how are we to avoid the conclusion that the
function of the liver is to produce sclerosis of the liver, given
that having the former is patently a necessary condition of
having the latter?*

*These sorts of problems have direct application at least
to certain kinds of theory construction in psychology. Suppose we attempt to explain some aspect of the behavior of an
organism by constructing a machine that simulates that behavior. Suppose, further, that we intend that, in the internal
organization of this machine, relays will play the role of
neurons: e.g., that the closing of a machine relay should correspond to the firing of an organic neuron, and so on. The
difficulty is to cash this equivocal "e.g." for a staunch "i.e."
Our intention is that, in this machine, the relays should fulfill
whatever functions the neuron fulfills in vivo—that the machine's relay should be functionally equivalent to the organism's neuron. But we cannot thereby require that every effect
of the neuron should also be an effect of the relay: that would
be to require that the relay be a neuron. What, then, is involved in requiring that the relay replicate precisely those of
the effects of a neuron that involve its function and no others?*

*It might be supposed that the following principle, at least,
can be taken for granted: if m_1 and m_2 are functionally equivalent mechanisms, and if $e_1, e_2, \ldots e_n$ are the series of
effects of m_1, then somewhere in that series there must be an
e_i such that $e_i \ldots e_n$ are effects of m_2. This, presumably,
is what we have in mind when we say of functionally equivalent systems that they do the same things. Functionally*

yes but, we can not really characterse
an event by E_i, that is this is itself based on
a classification scheme which itself is very complex

equivalent systems must somehow contrive, in the long run, to produce the same states of affairs.

Even this sort of suggestion is, however, relatively unhelpful for an attempt to clarify the concept of functional equivalence. For it appeals to a concept of "same state of affairs" that is unclear in much the same way that the notion of sameness of function is. Let us consider a concrete example, one not drawn from psychology.

Political theorists have often hypothesized that a policy of external aggression may serve a government in lieu of a policy of internal reform: either policy may lead to short-range domestic stability. That there is some point to this sort of suggestion recent American history amply testifies. The present question is whether we can capture the force of this hypothesis without abandoning strictly causal language. Notice that we have not done so if all that we have done is translate the hypothesis into the form: "Foreign aggression and domestic reform may each be nomologically sufficient for domestic stability." For we still require a purely causal analysis of the situations in which a society is properly said to be stable. There is, however, no reason to suppose that such an account can be given. Societies are stable when, for example, there exists widespread popular support for fundamental social institutions. But, now, the notion of a social institution is one that is typically functionally defined, and there exists no statement of the causally necessary and/or sufficient conditions a type of behavior must satisfy if it is to count as evincing support for a social institution.

In short, it looks, at first blush, as though we might find a path from talk about functional equivalences to the comfortingly causal talk characteristic of the hard sciences if we take functionally equivalent systems to be those whose effects are indistinguishable. But the appearance is misleading unless we have some reason to believe that the states of affairs upon *which functionally equivalent systems converge need not themselves be functionally defined. As things now stand, there is no particular reason to believe this.*

It may well turn out that there is no way of translating from "Q is the function of X" to "X is a causally necessary and/or sufficient condition for Q" and no way of translating from "P and R are functionally equivalent" to "P and R are each causal conditions for S" that will provide for the elimination of appeals to function and functional equivalences from the biological sciences. On the other hand, some such translation may be possible if appropriate constraints are placed upon the effects in terms of which functions are allowed to be defined. (Thus, it may be that only those effects of a biological structure that are adaptive, etc., count as its functions.) One way or the other, we require a careful analysis of the entailments of statements about functions, and this analysis ought not be constrained by the assumption that such statements can be cashed directly for statements about effects.

Prima facie, there is a relation between the question "What is the function of a mousetrap?" and the question "What is it to repair a mousetrap?" just as there is a relation between the question "What is the function of the heart?" and the question "What would a gadget have to do to be an artificial heart?" Talk about the function of Xs is, in short, related in a variety of ways to talk about artifical Xs, substitute Xs, impaired activity of Xs, pathological Xs, normal Xs, and so on and on. I suspect that working out the logic of this area of discourse is the right way of working out the constraints on functional analysis. There is gold in those hills.

I shall not, however, try to mine it here. I suspect that the problem of functional analysis is to be solved not by trying to reduce functions to effects, but rather by blocking out the implications of claims about functions. My present purpose, however, is simply to illustrate how such claims may be central to several aspects of psychological explanation. I am aware that to reduce one unsolved problem to another is not the limit of rational ambition. It may, nevertheless, be a way of getting started.

One final introductory remark. I am not inclined to believe that the language or the theories that scientists adopt are discontinuous with the language or theories of the nonscientific layman. The "language of science" is natural language; science is done, for example, in English and with the purpose (inter alia) *of explaining phenomena that have proved refractory to casual or unsystematic investigation. It therefore seems to me implausible in the extreme to represent the concepts and theories that psychologists use in their accounts of behavior as unrelated to, or as mere homonyms of, the concepts and theories in terms of which the layman's understanding of behavior is articulated. Insofar as attempting to solve the mind-body problem is, or involves, getting a clear view of the workings of mental terms in ordinary language, there is every reason to suppose that insight into that problem might be gained by a discussion of the functioning of the counterparts these terms have in scientific theories. It would be most desirable to arrive at an account of mental language that would work for both cases. In any event, it is a condition upon the way in which we understand the psychologist's use of "drive," "motive," "sensation," or whatever that the analysis should not render it logically impossible for psychological theories of drives, motives, and sensations sometimes to be solutions to the layman's questions about behavior. It is just such questions that psychological theories are, in the first instance, constructed in order to answer.*

Psychological Explanation

 ONE

Is Psychology Possible?

It is a point of definition that a science of psychology seeks to provide a systematic explanation of the behavior and of the behavioral capacities of organisms. In providing such explanations, psychologists have traditionally attempted to show that what an organism does is determined in some complicated way by specified features of its environment, on the one hand, and by its mental states, processes, events, operations, and so forth, on the other. The present chapter will examine, and finally reject, a number of philosophical arguments that purport to show that such attempts are necessarily conceptually incoherent.

Pragmatic Aspects of Explanation

I shall discuss only briefly those objections to the traditional program that depend upon maintaining that a systematic explanation of *anything* is impossible because, for example, to say that something needs to be explained is to imply that it is somehow untoward, abnormal, and unusual. On this account what is logically susceptible of explanation is a function of the expectations, beliefs, and norms of the inquirer so that a scientific theory counts as an explanation only for an inquirer whose beliefs, norms, and expectations are of the appropriate kinds. This is a view that has been widely held. It would, for example, seem to be the sort of thing Hamlyn has in mind when he asks:

What of explanations with regard to the veridical perception of the equality of length of a pair of lines seen under normal conditions? There is no question in this case that the lines might be expected to be seen as otherwise than of equal length. There is no question of a deviation from expectation, and if, nevertheless, some question were still asked beginning "Why ———," it must be a different sort of question from normal requests for explanation. For, explanation is normally called for when the phenomena are regarded, from a certain point of view, as unexpected.[1]

Grice has noted that such arguments are enthymemes and that the assumption they beg is very possibly false.[2] From the premise "To request an explanation of X is often to imply that X was unexpected" it is concluded that explanations of expected events are *logically* objectionable. But that conclusion follows only if it is also assumed that "X requires explanation" *logically* implies "X was unexpected." There are, of course, other possibilities. For example, the implication might be pragmatic (i.e., it might be carried by the speech act of requesting an explanation, rather than by the meaning of "explain").

The relevant difference between logical and pragmatic implication is that where "P implies Q" expresses a logical relationship, the expression "P and not Q" is self-contradictory. But in cases in which to say P implies Q pragmatically, the expression "P and not Q" is at worst bizarre, odd to say, and so forth. (Compare "He's a bachelor but he's married" with "He's a bachelor but I don't believe it.") But if "*P* and not *Q*" is logically consistent when *P* (only) pragmatically implies *Q*, and if we suppose that "It wants explaining, hence it's abnormal" expresses no more than a pragmatic implication, it follows that no *logical* incoherence attaches to demands for explanations of events that are not judged to be abnormal.

As Grice has pointed out, it is characteristic of merely pragmatic implications that it is possible to "cancel" them by choosing an appropriate form of words: that is, one that states explicitly that the implication is not intended to hold. For example, it is possible to say "I should like an explanation of *X*, even though I acknowledge that there is nothing abnormal or unexpected about *X* having occurred." If "*Y* wants *X* explained" pragmatically implies "*X* was unexpected for *Y*" we are ipso facto assured that the form of words just indicated is consistent. So it would appear that, at best, a proof that that implication is *not* (only) pragmatic is owing.[3]

However, a stronger point can be urged against Hamlyn than that his argument is inconclusive. For the claim that only exceptional phenomena are logically capable of being explained leads, in certain cases, to patent anomaly. Consider explaining why water beads on smooth surfaces like freshly waxed cars. Presumably the explanation would refer to the reciprocal relation between surface tension, which acts to form the fluid into a sphere, and friction, which tends to inhibit that action: in the "abnormal" case, the effects of the inhibitory force are relatively negligible. Note, however, that if we accept this explanation of the abnormal case, we are ipso facto committed to a corresponding explanation of the behavior of water in the "normal" case, in which water behaves in the way it is expected to behave (that is, in which it does *not* bead). In particular, if the abnormal case is the one in which the effects of friction can be discounted, the normal case is simply the one in which the effects of friction can *not* be discounted. If it is the absence of friction that explains the tendency of the fluid to approximate a sphere, then it is the presence of friction (and, of course, the action of gravity) that explains its tendency to approximate a plane. In short, the form of the explanation of a phenomenon that we regard as *un*usual implicitly determines the form of the explanation of what we take to be the typical case. We cannot, therefore, hold that the former case is logically capable of explanation and at the same time deny that the latter is too.

It is not difficult to see what must have led Hamlyn astray. It *is* true that to request an explanation of *X* is often to imply that one does not understand *X*. Now, among the reasons why one may not understand a phenomenon is the fact that it is unusual, rare, untoward, abnormal, or unexpected. Surely, however, this is not the only possible reason for lack of understanding, and to ignore the others is to fall victim to that obsessive concern with too few examples that Wittgenstein so much deplored. One may fail to understand a phenomenon because it is complicated (I do not understand why jet engines provide faster acceleration than conventional piston engines), or because it is apparently arbitrary (I do not understand why freely suspended bodies attract one another), or refractory to direct examination (I do not understand why the continents are arranged the way they are), or because it is in apparent contradiction to some general laws one believes should apply (I do not understand how quasars could pulse synchronously without violating relativistic limits). In each case (and, of course, this list is not nearly exhaustive), it is because one does not understand the phenomenon that one wants an explanation. But it is something other than abnormality of the phenomenon that accounts for one's failure to understand the phenomenon. Hence, in no such case can we deduce from the demand for explanation that the phenomenon is regarded as being abnormal.

The suggestion that demands for explanation presuppose a background of apparent abnormality in what is to be explained may be supposed to derive, in still another way, from a dearth of examples: in particular, from the philosophic habit of investigating those demands for explanation that take the form of "why-questions," almost to the exclusion of all others. For even if we grant (what seems to me patently absurd) that to ask "Why does the sun rise in the East?" is somehow to imply that the sun "ought" to rise in the West, we must bear in mind that *how*-questions are also often requests for explanation. And it is surely beyond belief that anyone would want to assert that a question like "How do internal-combustion engines work?" makes sense only against a background view that not working is their normal mode of functioning. Thus, even if Hamlyn were right about the impossibility of systematic theories being answers to questions that start "Why ————," that *might* show no more than that systematic psychological theories (*inter alia*) ought to be construed as answers to questions that start "How ————," for example, "How do we perceive things?" "How do we solve problems?" "How do we form concepts?" and "How do we learn things?"

It is, of course, a historical fact that psychologists have often been professionally interested in such cases of patent abnormality as perceptual illusion. There are, however, no grounds for attempting to convert this fact into a methodological canon. Psychologists who have interested themselves in illusions and analogous phenomena have done so not because their science is inherently concerned with the analysis of deviations but simply because a concern with illusions is the natural consequence of the application of the method of differences to the study of *normal* perception.

Suppose, for example, that you suspect that the detection of texture gradients is normally a sufficient cue for the perception of visual depth. A natural way of testing this hypothesis is to construct a *two*-dimensional stimulus on which texture gradient is varied while other putative depth cues are controlled. If your hypothesis about the role of texture gradient in depth perception is right, a two-dimensional stimulus on which texture gradients are appropriately deployed should appear to be (i.e., *should give the illusion of being*) three-dimensional. Hence, if you are a psychologist interested in the role of texture gradients in normal space perception, you are, almost willy-nilly, a psychologist interested in the ability of texture gradients to produce spatial illusions. But that does *not* mean that, qua psychologist, illusions are your primary objects of study. To produce a ϕ illusion by the manipulation of some variable *may* be to demonstrate the role of that variable in nonillusory ϕ perception. Hence, the study of illusions and other sorts of exceptional phenomena is an occasional stratagem of the psychology of perception.

The Scope of Psychological Theories

Let us now return to psychological explanations. We said that the general goal of such explanations is to show how the behavior of an organism is a function of environmental variables and mental operations. But it must be admitted that this formulation of the goal is unclear in a number of respects, and it is important to determine which, if any, of these unclarities gives ground for philosophical concern. For example, it is evident that "behavior" is being put to a technical use when it is employed as a general term for the domain of psychological investigations; nor is it entirely clear how this employment is to be understood or what phenomena the term is intended to cover. Since the psychologist is willing to regard dreaming and problem solving as cases of behaving, it is apparent that in his usage "behavior" has lost the connotation of "deportment," which, some dictionaries say, is characteristic of its use in ordinary language. Yet the psychologist cannot wish to say that the behavior of an organism includes literally everything the organism does. It demands psychological explanation that there are conditions under which an organism ignores visual cliffs, but it is no part of psychology to explain why the organism that does so sometimes falls. Analogously, it may be the psychologist's duty to predict when a person will speak, but it is presumably not part of the program to predict when he will sneeze.

This sort of unclarity is harmless, however, since it can plausibly be attributed to that beast of all burdens, the "immaturity of the behavioral sciences."

In their early development, sciences are often identifiable by their concern with explaining some quite specific set of phenomena. Just as current experimental psychology is primarily the study of learning and perception, so astronomy was initially the attempt to provide an orderly account of the motions of the stars and planets, and genetics began with theories of family resemblance. But though theories in a young science may be produced in order to deal with a relatively specific set of phenomena, they are evaluated in part by their broader implications. *Ceteris paribus,* theories are accepted when they yield insight into problems that they were not specifically designed to solve. The new phenomena, so explained, are thereby brought into the domain of the science, which, in effect, grows by a process of assimilation. Cases of this sort are ubiquitous in the history of science.

For example, the two-sphere universe was initially developed principally to account for the diurnal motions of the stars and for the way in which those motions varied with the observer's location on the earth. But once it had been developed, the new theory was readily extended to give order and simplicity to observations of the sun's motions as well. And, having disclosed the unsuspected regularities that underlie the complexity of the sun's behavior, the conceptual scheme provided a framework within which could be studied the even more irregular motions of the planets.[4]

In short, the conceptual mechanisms employed by a science amount to an implicit specification of what it means for phenomena to be similar in theoretically relevant respects; they thereby determine which kinds of phenomena the science is responsible for explaining. It is when we have a theory of mechanics that we are brought to take note of the similarity between the behavior of the moon and the behavior of a projectile. A theory of evolution exhibits the similarity between the differentiation of song in birds and the differentiation of their sexual coloration. A theory of language shows the respect in which grammaticality and ambiguity are properties of the same logical character. In each case, an important argument in favor of accepting the theory which exhibits those similarities is that it permits us to greatly extend the domain of a science without having to pay the price of a vast complication of its conceptual equipment.

There is, then, an important sense in which a science has to discover what it is about: it does so by discovering that the laws and concepts it produced in order to explain one set of phenomena can be fruitfully applied to phenomena of other sorts as well. It is thus only in retrospect that we can say of all the phenomena embraced by a single theoretical framework that *they* are what we meant, for example, by the presystematic term "physical event," or "chemical inter-action," or "behavior." To the extent that such terms, or their employments, are neologistic, the neologism is occa-sioned by the insights that successful theories provide into the deep similarities that underlie superficially heterogeneous events.

These remarks are relevant to an objection that is often raised against the possibility of systematic psychological theories—namely, that not every action under every descrip-tion could fall within their domain. Sometimes the hand that signs a paper fells a city. But it is not clear, in such cases, which, if either, event the psychologist is obliged to explain.

It is, however, no use suggesting, as some philosophers have done,[5] that considerations such as these preclude a psychology that is general vis-à-vis behavior in the same sense as that in which the other special sciences are supposed to be general with respect to their domains. For precisely the same sort of point could be made against the generality of physical explanation or, for that matter, of any type of explanation. Suppose I purchase a sketch. Is this a physical transaction (objects were displaced, forces exerted), or an economic one (I spent more than I could afford), or is it perhaps an aesthetic one because I took the sketch that seemed to me to have the warmest shading? At best it is a physical transaction *inter alia*—that is, under a certain de-scription—as a sunset is, or an earthquake, or the explosion of a nuclear bomb. Perhaps, then, what is required in order for *physics* to be general is that, for each event, there be *some* description in terms of physical magnitudes. But this suggestion is possibly too strong and certainly unclear, since it inherits and carries forward the vagueness of presystematic criteria for individuating events. At 2:00 A.M. we go on day-light-saving time. Is what happens at 2:00 A.M. a physical event? And, if there is no clear answer to this sort of question, must we therefore abandon the search for physical theories for which generality can be claimed?

Such questions seem artificial in the case of physics, precisely because, given a physical theory, it is possible to see what sort of things it ought to explain and under which descriptions it ought to explain them. Hence given such a theory it is possible to see what would constitute a serious counterexample to its putative generality. Here again the relevant point is that the properties a phenomenon must have in order to fall within the domain of the theory are specified ex post facto by reference to the conceptual mechanisms that the theory employs. Since such mechanisms implicitly define what generality would mean *for that sort of theory,* the question whether the theory is general in some more metaphysical (and less clear) sense need not be regarded as pressing.

In short, among the advantages that ought to accrue to the development of a systematic account of behavior is a clear demarcation of the sorts of phenomena that a theory of behavior ought to be required to explain. In terms of such a clarification, serious questions could be raised about the extent to which behavioral theories either succeed or fail to be general. But there is no a priori basis for denying generality to behavioral theories that does not also hold for claims to generality for other branches of science, nor does the notion of generality at issue appear to be clearer in one case than in the other.

Ontological Status of Psychological Constructs

I have argued that while a certain vagueness does attach to the psychologist's notion of behavior, that fact affords no grounds for philosophical objections to the claim that the systematic explanation of behavior is an appropriate goal for psychological inquiry. It is evident that a similar unclarity attaches to the term "mental," insofar as the psychologist formulates his objective as the explanation of behavior by reference to mental events and processes. But I think it is arguable that, though this usage leaves certain important questions open, their resolution is largely independent of the truth of the empirical assertions that psychological theories make.

In the sense of "mental" in which it is correct to say that psychologists have traditionally assumed that behavior must be explained by reference to mental events, it is clear that mentalism must be opposed to behaviorism rather than to physicalism. We shall return to this point at length in Chapter II. Suffice it to remark here that what psychologists who have as little else in common as Freud, Lorenz, and Hull have all maintained, and what only some American learning theorists appear to deny, is that explanations of behavior must employ nonlogical terms whose referents are not themselves bits of behavior or classes of bits of behavior. When psychologists accuse one another of mentalism, it is the proliferation of theoretical constructs, rather than of types of substance, that they are usually objecting to.

It is possible to deny that all psychological terms denote observables while at the same time refusing to speculate about the ultimate nature of the entities that the theoretical terms in psychological explanations do refer to. It is even arguable that there is some precedent for refusing to be explicit about what one is studying prior to the conclusion of the study. Thus, a psychologist who admits that he is unclear about the ontological status of the drives, motives, and so forth that populate his theories might argue that ignorance of the nature of genes was compatible with the development of a quite satisfactory science of genetics. The geneticist could afford to be neutral among various theories about the nature of trait-bearing entities and the details of their operation, because his evidence permitted him to determine when theoretically relevant relations hold between those entities, as well as what observable consequences their interactions have. This information turned out to be adequate for the construction of a systematic account of trait transmission. Note that it was not merely the precise biochemistry of the gene that was unknown to early students of heredity. Even such apparently ontological questions as whether the unit of heredity is an "entity" remained open until Mendel's classic demonstration that recessive characteristics appear unaltered in the offspring of heterozygotes. Since it was this demonstration that showed that a distinction is required between traits and their genetic carriers, it was only in light of Mendel's work that the geneticist could confidently assert that the primary object of his study is the interaction of trait-bearing *entities* rather than the interaction of *traits*.

In light of such historical precedents, many psychologists are inclined to waive questions about the nature of the mental events they postulate in explanations of behavior, so long as their data permit them to certify systematic relations among such events, as well as between them and the behavior that they produce. It is, on this view, unnecessary to say what a drive is, so long as we can say when one is reduced and what are the behavioral consequences of its reduction. With drives as with genes, the initial question is what they *do,* not what they *are*.

At first glance, this position may appear modest to the point of invulnerability. It is difficult to argue against the propriety of explaining behavior by reference to mental events, as long as the burden of the qualifier "mental" is left unspecified. That is why arguments against dualism in the Cartesian sense leave many psychologists cold. How, indeed, *could* the metaphysical questions engage the scientific ones?

Perhaps, then, the psychologist can say all that he needs to say without committing himself on how many kinds of substance there are. Nevertheless, if psychological explanations are to be like explanations in other sciences, it is essential that the entities they refer to should be susceptible of the sorts of categorial ascriptions generally characteristic of theoretical entities. Such terms as "cause," "effect," and "event" must, in short, be predicable of what the psychologist studies, if his explanations are to have the character of scientific theories. The novelty of recent philosophical discussions of psychology is that they maintain that the application of such predicates to motives, reasons, and feelings constitutes an instance of categorical misascription. The emphasis is thus shifted from arguing that the objection to "mental events" is that they are supposed to be mental to arguing that the objection to mental events is that they are supposed to be events.

It is widely held among philosophers that even such apparently innocent locutions as "perceptual process" or "the motive that caused him to act as he did," or "mental event" itself are pregnant with conceptual confusion, and that the elaborate theories of motivation, volition, perception, and so forth, that some philosophers and many psychologists have embraced are best understood as extensions of the semi-grammatical errors embodied in such locutions. A theory of the perceptual processes *must be* a mistaken theory: "perceive" is not a process word. If it is indeed a logical truth that perceiving is not a process at all, then no psychological theory can ever throw light on *what sort of* process it is. By analogy, a theory of the psychological causation of behavior must be mistaken inasmuch as what psychological terms designate are ipso facto not causes: if it is indeed a logical truth that a motive is not a cause, then no psychological theory can hope to explain *how* motives cause behavior.

Here, then, is an area in which the vagueness admittedly implicit in the notion of a systematic psychology courts disaster. It will not do in such cases as these to plead that empirical progress will help clarify the methodological issues or that inquiry can proceed without such clarification, for the charge to be answered is precisely that no progress is possible where the problems under investigation are unreal. It is now necessary to review a number of the main arguments upon which this sort of charge is based.

Let us begin with perception and, in particular, with some questions that a psychologist might suppose to be paradigmatic of those that a theory of perception ought to be able to answer—for example, "How do we see robins?" or "How do we recognize 'Lillibullero'?" We shall see presently why a psychologist might think these questions hard; at this point, we want to see what can be said for the view that they are senseless.

It might be argued, to begin with, that "perceive" and "recognize" denote achievements of a kind. In typical cases, that is, it is the presence of a robin or the fact that it *is* "Lillibullero" that the orchestra is playing that makes the difference between perceiving and recognizing, on one hand, and misperceiving and failing to recognize, on the other. Hence it is to facts about what is on the lawn or facts about what is being played—and not to pseudo-facts about covert mental processes—that we must refer when questions about either perception or misperception arise.

Now, it is maintained that psychologists have usually understood such questions as "How do we perceive?" and "How do we recognize?" precisely as demands for the enumeration of some mental events whose occurrence serves to distinguish perceiving from misperceiving and recognizing from failing to recognize. But since it is facts that are logically analogous to the presence of robins that account for that

can do ask
"what are whens" ie
what is in tort of the
class of objects is

distinction, it follows that there could be no such mental
events. Hence, it is argued, the sorts of questions just instanced
ought to be abandoned or rephrased in a less misleading logical style. As Ryle says, the kinds of questions it is reasonable
to ask about perception are not "questions of the para-me-
chanical form 'How do we see robins?', but questions of the
form 'How do we use such descriptions as "He saw a
robin"?' " [6] But if there is no reasonable question one can
ask about how robins are perceived, there must surely be
something wrong with the theories that psychologists have
proposed in order to answer such questions. [7]

What precisely does this argument show? Grant that
what makes the difference between actually perceiving a
robin and incorrectly supposing oneself to have done so is
that, in cases of the first sort, a robin must be present. That
is, grant that the presence of a robin is a *necessary* condition for the perception of a robin. Since it is patent that it is
not also a *sufficient* condition, may not a psychologist argue
as follows: given a robin to be perceived, what determines
whether it *is* perceived is the occurrence of certain mental
events? That is, might it not be maintained that while the
presence of a robin may make the difference between perceiving a robin and incorrectly believing oneself to have perceived one, it is the occurrence of the relevant mental events
that makes the difference between perceiving robins *inter alia*
and not perceiving anything at all. To put it slightly differently, the argument so far is compatible with the view that
the presence of a robin and the occurrence of certain mental
events are singly necessary and jointly sufficient for perceiving
a robin. If this were correct, there would be some point to
the psychologist's attempt to say what the relevant mental
events are.

This argument would be beside the point, of course, if
we were to suppose that a psychological theory of perception

is an attempt to enumerate only the *logically* necessary conditions for perceiving robins. But it would be absurd to suppose that psychological accounts of the functioning of the perceptual mechanisms are intended to be necessarily true, or that psychologists and epistemologists hold their paramechanical remarks to be analytic. Even Kant maintained that his theory of perception was certified by an analysis of experience, not by an analysis of the term "experience," and Hume held that the difference between sensation and perception is the consequence of thoroughly contingent principles of association. Nor need one argue, I suppose, for the claim that a psychologist who holds the detection of texture gradients to be necessary for monocular depth perception should not be understood to have embraced a necessary proposition.

It is, however, precisely the absurd view that all relevant psychological truths about mental processes are necessary truths that we are led to if we follow Ryle's advice and substitute inquiries into how we use locutions that assert that a performance has come off for inquiries into those mechanisms whose functioning is essential to the performance. For, given the way in which philosophers use "use," investigations of the first kind must arrive at necessary truths if they arrive at any truths at all. "X perceived a robin entails that there was a robin X perceived" is presumably a paradigm of an analytic statement, and its being so is clearly prerequisite to its relevance to the conceptual inquiry into use that Ryle commends. Thus the systematic substitution of questions about how we use "perceive" for questions about the mechanisms of perception makes it appear that there is nothing to be said about perceiving except what is logically akin to the necessary truth just cited, and hence that there is nothing for an empirical theory of perception to be about, no body of contingent truths for such a theory to articulate. The trick consists in establishing the conviction that questions about when it is appropriate to use certain descriptions are somehow (*just* how is never indicated) preferable alternatives to the "paramechanical" questions unreconstructed psychologists are wont to ask. From this one infers that, since it is only logical inquiries that correspond to questions of the former sort, there are no empirical inquiries that correspond to questions of the latter sort.

Ryle says:

> We do not . . . want tidings or hypotheses about any other things which the listener may have privily done or undergone. Even if there had taken place three, or seventeen, such *entr'actes,* news about them would not explain how detecting a mosquito differs from having a shrill singing in the ears. What we want to know is how the logical behavior of "he detected a mosquito" differs from that of "there was a singing in his ears," from that of "he tried in vain to make out what was making the noise," and from that of "he mistook it for the noise of the wind in the telephone wires." [8]

As an expression of taste these remarks are, of course, unimpeachable. They provide insight into the difference between the kind of inquiry proper to psychology and the kind of conceptual analysis philosophers pursue. The trouble arises when it is suggested that one sort of study ought somehow to replace the other; that inquiry into the use of mental terms is a saner form of the empirical research that psychologists undertake and that its pertinency is grounds for abandonment of psychological theories of perception and the paramechanics that they employ. That is, trouble arises if expressions of taste are treated as though they were arguments. How much trouble arises becomes evident if Ryle's suggestion is translated into a domain about which our intuitions are clearer. I want to argue that a single-minded adherence to Ryle's suggestion suffices to eliminate as conceptually disreputable not only "paramechanics" but also automotive mechanics, and this surely shows that something has gone wrong.

Consider the following parody on Ryle's procedure. We

suggest first that "function," when applied to an internal-combustion engine, is a "success" verb in that we use it to report that the behavior of the engine satisfies the norms, standards, and so forth commonly applied in evaluating the behavior of engines. But then it follows immediately that a theory of *how* engines function (that is, of the mechanical transactions that determine the difference between functioning and malfunctioning) must invariably be a howler since, by hypothesis, it is the satisfaction of norms and standards that determines that difference. How, then, are we to avoid blundering into the pseudo-science of automotive mechanics? How are we to avoid the grammatical misapprehensions that tempt us to seek mechanical explanations of the behavior of engines? We must systematically replace misleading questions like "How do engines work?" with antiseptic questions like "How do we use such descriptions as 'This engine worked last Tuesday'?"

Upon analysis, two relevant facts emerge. The first is that such descriptions as "This engine worked last Tuesday" hold only when certain hypotheticals are true. For example, for it to be true that this engine worked last Tuesday, it must be true that, *ceteris paribus,* if the accelerator had been depressed last Tuesday while the ignition was on, the angular velocity of the wheels would thereupon have increased. Second, it appears that the double implication "If this engine worked last Tuesday then, *ceteris paribus,* if the accelerator had been depressed while the ignition was on, the angular velocity of the wheels would thereupon have increased" is in some sense a truth of logic, for *that* its output increases when additional fuel is supplied is part of what we mean to say when we say of an engine that it works. But notice that if this is a truth of logic, it is ipso facto not a candidate for a truth of the pseudo-science of automotive mechanics. Since similar reasoning will apply to all answers to questions about how the description "This engine worked last Tuesday" and its logical kin are employed, and since such questions have, *ex hypothesis,* been everywhere substituted for questions about *how* engines work, it follows that there is nothing for an empirical science of automotive mechanics to be about. Hence we need not assume, in our speculations about the behavior of automobiles, that "Some special but unobserved ghostly wheels had gone round, wheels whose existence and functions only epistemologists [read 'automobile mechanics'] are clever enough to diagnose." [9]

The paradox is, of course, thoroughly contrived. In the case of automobiles, at least, it is perfectly clear that inquiring into the conditions under which it is appropriate to say "It works" (e.g., inquiring into the norms, standards, etc., a working engine is required to satisfy) is quite different from inquiring *how* it works, so the suggestion that we abandon the latter sort of inquiry in favor of the former is utterly gratuitous. It was only when we pretended to take that suggestion seriously that it began to seem that there could be no body of empirical facts for automotive mechanics to explain.

There are a number of replies that might be made. It might, for example, be suggested that the question about how we perceive things and the question about how automobiles work differ in at least the following way: while the latter question "points to" a mechanical explanation in a way that makes clear what sort of answer would be pertinent, the former question seems not to determine the form of its answer in any such fashion. Hence one question is unclear in a way in which the other is not.

It seems evident, however, that if "How do automobiles work?" appears to point to a mechanical answer, that is only because we know that mechanical theories do in fact provide satisfactory explanations of the workings of automobiles. If automobiles grew wild instead of being artifacts, the question how they worked would, when first asked, be as far from determining a mechanical answer as, say, the question "How do flowers grow?" is now.[10] Or to take a classic case, unclear questions, such as "What is burning?" "How do things burn?" or "What makes things burn?" have occasionally turned out to have a variety of clear answers, some of the most interesting of which are of a type that was surely unanticipated when such questions were first raised. The answer that the question "What makes something burn?" *obviously* demands (viz., "heat") *now* strikes one as no better than facetious.

It might also be suggested that since statements about how perception works do not, on the present view, express necessary truths, an enumeration of the mental operations that are ingredient in perception might be relevant to psychological theories, but would not be relevant to philosophical ones. I am not entirely unsympathetic to this suggestion, and since I know of no form of philosophical discussion more tedious or less rewarding than the border dispute, I shall not wrangle over what is at any event a preemptive definition. Nor is it necessary to do so in the present case. For the point of Ryle's argument is clearly not to save philosophy from mentalism by mere stipulation. It is evident that a behavioristic philosophy of mind would not satisfy Ryle if it had to be purchased at the cost of a mentalistic psychology.

The following line of rebuttal is, I think, more interesting: "Granted that some mental transactions may be ingredient in perception, let us see whether or not we can specify them. It is presumably a sufficient condition for someone to have perceived a thing, first, that the thing was there to be perceived and, second, that the perceiver should have entertained certain sensations and certain expectations. Therefore, if we are going to posit 'gears going around' when we perceive something, they must not, on pain of Occam's razor, be more complicated than would be required to explain the formation of the relevant sensations and expectations. And, surely, some rather simple story about learned associations will explain the latter. Hence, insofar as a psychological theory is supposed to account for nonsensory processes in perception, quite a little theory will probably do."

This in fact appears to be very close to the story Ryle has to tell.

> In short, he is now recognizing or following the tune if, knowing how it goes, he is now using that knowledge; and he uses that knowledge not just by hearing the tune, but by hearing it in a special frame of mind, the frame of mind of being ready to hear both what he is now hearing and what he will hear, or would be about to hear, if the pianist continues playing it and is playing it correctly.[11]

Ryle also provides a disarmingly informal discussion of the sorts of expectation that, if exhibited, would count as supporting the claim that the tune had been recognized.

> . . . he will be said to recognize it, when he hears it, if he does any, some or all of the following things: if, after hearing a bar or two, he expects those bars to follow which do follow; if he does not erroneously expect the previous bars to be repeated; if he detects omissions or errors in the performance; if, after the music has been switched off for a few moments, he expects it to resume where it does resume; if, when several people are whistling different tunes, he can pick out who is whistling this tune; if he can beat time correctly; if he can accompany it by whistling or humming it in time and tune, and so on indefinitely.[12]

As he makes clear elsewhere, Ryle thinks that recognizing a tune involves hearing it "according to a recipe." And lest this sound as though the notion of a recipe is being made to do the kind of work that concepts do in more familiar accounts, Ryle is willing to emphasize that talk about recipes can be converted into the "hard cash" of talk about hypotheticals.

That a person is following a tune is, if you like, a fact both about his ears and about his mind, but it is not a conjunction of one fact about his ears and another fact about his mind, or a conjoint report of one incident in his sensitive life and another incident in his intellectual life. It is what I have called a "semi-hypothetical," or "mongrel-categorical," statement.[13]

Nor is it only elaborate theories of perception that this view renders otiose. Theories of learning of any degree of complexity also go by the board.

There is no more of an epistemological puzzle involved in describing how infants learn perception recipes than there is in describing how boys learn to bicycle. They learn by practice, and we can specify the sorts of practice that expedite this learning.[14]

At this point, both psychologist and epistemologist might argue with justice that the appealing simplicity of Ryle's position is purchased by begging precisely the sorts of question that theories of perception and of learning have traditionally attempted to answer. Suppose we admit it to be a logical truth that someone who recognizes a rendition of "Lillibullero" must be entertaining certain expectations, and suppose we pretend for the moment that this analysis of recognizing into sensing and expecting can be made general. It would certainly appear to be reasonable to request that such an account say what, precisely, the relevant expectations are. To put it differently, it is reasonable to address to a theory that identifies recognizing a tune with hearing it according to a recipe the request that it publish the recipe.

But no sooner is that request taken seriously than all the classical arguments for conceptualism come trooping back. Consider, in particular, the "recipe" for hearing "Lillibullero"; consider, that is, what a person has to know in order to be able to recognize renditions of "Lillibullero."

It is clear, in the first place, that the set of events that one is capable of easily recognizing as a performance of "Lillibullero" need not have any distinguishing acoustic characteristics. In fact, no two members of that set need have such characteristics in common. For one can recognize the tune when it is played on a warped record, transposed, played as a waltz, played as a march, and so on and on. It is important to bear in mind that, from a strictly acoustical point of view, the capacity to identify the tune in these various guises amounts to an enormous but highly specific tolerance of distortion. On the one hand, to recognize a tune played at half speed on a phonograph with the volume turned down is to be able to recognize it in spite of the simultaneous alteration of pitch, amplitude, and temporal relations. On the other hand, certain mathematically trivial transformations of the tune (such as turning it upside down) render it completely unrecognizable for any except highly sophisticated listeners. It goes without saying that current work in artificial intelligence is not within miles of being able to build a computer that exhibits comparable perceptual characteristics.[15]

The present example is, of course, in no way special. A large number of the things one can recognize, such as shapes, tunes, sentences, and faces are drawn from stimulus domains that have quite complex mathematical structures. Invariably, in these cases, one's perceptual capacity includes the ability instantaneously and spontaneously to correct for quite gross distortions *of certain strictly determined kinds.* Cubes look like cubes however they may be rotated. Faces look like faces whether they are smiling or frowning, whether they are upside down or rightside up, whether they are seen in profile or full on; "A Hard Day's Night" sounds like "A Hard Day's Night," even when it is played by a baroque ensemble.

Any serious attempt to construct a viable psychological theory of perception would have to account for this sort of tolerance; that is, it would have to account for the fact that training often generalizes to objects that may be only quite abstractly related to the trained object. I cannot imagine how this is to be done unless it is assumed that the concept you have of a face, or a tune, or a shape (i.e., one's "recipe for recognizing" shapes, tunes, and faces) includes a representation of the formal structure of each of these domains and that the act of recognition involves the application of such information to the integration of current sensory inputs.

What one has to know in order to be able to recognize a tune in all its various transmutations is thus something more abstract than a specification of the absolute tonal, or acoustic, or temporal values of a series of notes. In particular, one does not need to be taught for *each* of the possible ways of rendering "Lillibullero" that it *is* a way of rendering "Lillibullero," for there are indefinitely many ways of doing the thing, and if one had to learn them all in turn, one would never finish learning.

(It won't do, of course, to say that what the various performances of "Lillibullero" have in common is a family resemblance and that learning the recipe is learning to recognize that resemblance. For while that is quite true, it is only a way of reformulating the fact that needs to be explained—viz., that when we have learned to recognize "Lillibullero," we have learned to hear as similar what may be physically quite different sequences of tones.)

In short, if what the various ways of performing "Lillibullero" have in common is something abstract, then it would appear to follow that the system of expectations that constitutes one's recipe for hearing the song must be abstract in the same sense. For, on the present account, it is the fact that one has and applies the recipe that explains, *inter alia,* one's ability to recognize novel renditions of the tune. And now it begins to look as though the notion of expectation that Ryle works with is unclear in a way that allows him to beg some vital issues. For what precisely *is* one expecting when one is expecting the next note to be such and such? Not, again, some particular tonal value, for I can play "Lillibullero" *en collage,* for example, by having the first note performed by an orchestra, the second whistled, the third played by an oboe, and so forth. And it will still be a rendition of "Lillibullero," —that is, the surprise of the hearer would not be the sort of surprise he would have experienced had I played the first twelve notes of "Lillibullero" and then followed this with the first ten bars of the Second Movement of Haydn's Symphony No. 94. In both cases, expectations would be defeated but, in the latter case, they are not the ones that are logically connected with recognizing "Lillibullero."

If, then, knowing the recipe is to be identified with being disposed to entertain certain expectations, it is evident that these expectations will have to be of a very abstract sort. For, insofar as dramatic differences in their absolute values are compatible with two performances both being renditions of "Lillibullero," such differences must be compatible with the satisfaction of whatever expectations are logically connected with the "Lillibullero" recipe. Having the recipe must be very much more like having the sheet music than like having the record.

Indeed, Ryle very nearly gives the show away when he mentions "expecting those bars to follow which do follow . . . beating time correctly . . . etc." as among those performances that would indicate that a tune has been recognized. For of course one *can* give some account of the information the hearer must employ in recognizing a tune, if one allows oneself such notions as "bar," "note," "measure," and "tempo." This is hardly surprising since such notions have developed precisely in the context of attempts to provide a vocabulary that is abstract enough to represent the common features of acoustically different renditions of a tune; they represent a more or less explicit theory of the type/token relation for music. Since, however, these musicological concepts *are* abstract (that is, since they have, by and large, no simple acoustic interpretation), to admit that they are required to describe the perceptual recipes for tunes is simply to admit that learning to recognize tunes involves internalizing and applying complex concepts—presumably as the result of correspondingly complex mental operations.

Moreover, if the recipe for recognizing "Lillibullero" must be abstract in order to account for the recognizability of the tune in its sundry possible manifestations, it presumably follows that the mental operations involved in *applying* the recipe must be correspondingly complex. For which note in particular (i.e., which absolute values of key, duration, intensity, stress, pitch, amplitude, etc.) we expect after hearing the first few notes of a performance of "Lillibullero" will depend not only upon the recipe but also upon the particular characteristics of those first notes. And, although the defeat of *this* expectation may be compatible with recognizing the tune, as we have seen, it is *not* compatible with following *this* rendition of the tune. Hence, the formation of such expectations (presumably by integration of the recipe with information about tonal, temporal, and so on, constants of the present performance) is something that an account of perception will need complex theoretical mechanisms to explain.

It thus appears that, once the recipe story is made explicit, it is indistinguishable from a quite elaborate conceptualism. That is, it is unclear how to account for the ability to recognize identity of type despite gross variation among tokens unless we assume that the concepts employed in recognition are of formidable abstractness. But then it is unclear how the *application* of such concepts (or, of course, their assimilation) is to be explained, unless one assumes psychological mechanisms whose operations must be complicated in the extreme.

Once this has been understood there is, of course, no harm in insisting upon what is by now a philosophical platitude—namely, that talk about perception recipes, like talk about any other theoretical construct, is, in principle, equivalent to talk about infinite sets of hypotheticals. Insofar as it seeks to account for behavior, a psychological theory may be thought of as a function that maps an infinite set of possible inputs to an organism onto an infinite set of possible outputs. Such a function, like any other, may be treated in extension, which is to say that any psychological account of behavior is equivalent to an infinite set of hypotheticals, whose antecedents denote input states and whose consequents denote output states. Indeed, it is in large part because infinitely many hypotheticals are true of the behavior of any organism that psychological theories are necessary; otherwise, the behavioral repertoire of an organism could in principle be represented by a list. It must be added, moreover, that there is no obvious reason why we should be more inclined to think of perception recipes (concepts) as requiring elimination in favor of such hypotheticals than electrons, magnetic fields, quasars, or, for that matter, tables and chairs.

Thus far, I have assumed an analysis of recognizing into sensing and expecting. I have pointed out that, on that analysis, the relevant expectations must be complex and abstract on the ground that perceptual identities are often surprisingly independent of the existence of physical uniformities among stimuli. Since it is precisely in order to explain this perceptual "constancy" that psychologists and epistemologists have traditionally supposed that unconscious inferences and other paramechanical transactions will be needed, it seems relevant to remark that Ryle's treatment has begged all the issues that such constancy raises.

It is, however, not only the expecting that turns out to be

problematical. For it appears that the type/token relation is quite as abstract for "objects of sensation" as it is for objects of perception. Consider the prima facie trivial problems that are involved in accounting for the recognition of speech sounds by a native speaker of a language. Here talk of expectations is likely to be otiose since it is not evident what system of expectations could be logically relevant to the difference between, say, recognizing a sound as an utterance of /t/ and recognizing it as an utterance of /p/. What is interesting is that it is equally unapparent what acoustic differences could account for this sort of discrimination. For it appears upon careful investigation that the naïve psychophysics according to which sensory differences are uniformly attributable to isomorphic physical differences does not hold true for this case. Whatever may be the distinguishing characteristic that all the utterances of a given English consonant have in common, it is certainly not some acoustic feature.

In the case of speech perception, then, recognition of the elements apparently exhibits the same sort of independence from the physical properties of the input as recognition of the sequences of elements does in the perception of tunes. And, while I am far from wishing to attribute psychophysical views to Ryle, if the perceptual identity of utterances of /t/s cannot be explained by reference to their acoustic identity, it seems clear that some mental processing will have to be assumed instead. To put the point succinctly, if, as all the evidence suggests,[16] the equivalence of /t/s is a *learned* equivalence, a psychological theory will be required to say precisely what is learned, how it is learned, and how what has been learned is applied by someone who can tell a /t/ when he hears one. The current state of the art is that no one can approximate a satisfactory answer to any of these questions. Yet unless he can provide such answers, and in a way that avoids mentalistic postulations, Ryle's reference to sensing in his analysis of perception as sensing and expecting would appear to be quite as tendentious as we have found his notion of expectation to be. The mental operations that Ryle attempted to sweep under the rug are (to mix a metaphor) about to turn up at the back door.

It may be remarked that Ryle's aside about the transparency of the learning process is susceptible to equally serious objections: the outstanding questions are neither solved nor dissolved; they are merely begged. *Of course* it is true that we know what conditions are normally empirically sufficient for learning to ride a bicycle. The difficulty is, first, that we do not know what conditions are *necessary* and, second, that we do not know what learning principles account for the facility that humans display in mastering this sort of task. Thus it is by no means obvious that the forms of tuition in which parents indulge when they "teach" their child to ride (or, for that matter, to walk) have, in fact, much value in facilitating the learning. And it is even less obvious why the loose schedule of training that eventuates in a human being able to ride a bicycle (or talk a language) will not work with a dog.

One does not have an account of learning when one knows only that a sufficient condition for a child learning to swim is that he be placed in the water and told to paddle. Nor is it illuminating to say that the learning depends on practice, since the puzzle consists precisely in explaining what it is about one's crude splashing that makes *it* practice for the finished performance. It is tempting to answer that question either by referring to the intensional character of practicing, or by holding that it is in some sense an a priori truth that doing just *this* counts as practicing for such and such. Neither such move will work. Although it is true that practicing requires behaving with a certain end in view, it is equally true that having the appropriate intentions will by no means guarantee that one is practicing. What counts as practicing depends upon what, in fact, normally facilitates learning, and this depends in turn upon what laws of learning exist. Analogously, it is implausible to argue that it is a fact of logic (i.e., part of the meaning of "practice") that one normally practices complicated performances by producing relatively crude approximations of them. It is not difficult to imagine a world in which the assimilation of complex skills is contingent upon the performance of actions that are quite different from those involved in the skilled performance. Even in our world one may practice for a concert by playing scales, although one has no intention of playing scales in the concert hall.

Psychological Explanations and Causal Explanations

There is a line of argument I have avoided so far, that I shall now have to examine. "Granted that the above considerations appear to require the occurrence of some complicated processes when things are perceived. Granted, that is, that when I perceive a thing there is a complicated story to be told about what is happening in my nervous system. Nevertheless, that is a story about causal transactions and is thus evidently not a story that the psychologist's conceptual equipment permits him to tell. For reasons, motives, drives, impulses, and so on are paradigms of the sorts of constructs in terms of which psychological explanations are articulated, and it is clear upon analysis that such constructs cannot appear in the role of causes."

This is a serious argument, not only because it would have the effect of driving a wedge between psychology and the other sciences, but also because, if it is correct, then all attempts to establish relations of contingent identity between psychological and neurological constructs must necessarily fail. Since neurological events are precisely the sorts of things that are involved in causal transactions, it is a condition upon their identifiability with psychological events that causal predicates should also be applicable to the latter.

On the question of whether the theoretical terms in psychological theories could designate causes (e.g., of behavior), two arguments must be examined, the first of which is not serious.

It is plausible to say of some actions that the logical possibility of their performance requires an agent to be in a certain state or condition. Hence, in explanations of behavior, both laymen and psychologists often have reason to advert to states whose presence or absence determines what action a performance instances. For example, it is patent that one cannot be guilty of telling a lie unless one believes what one says to be false; that is, that behavior that counts as lying in a man who believes that what he says is false would not do so in the case of a man who believes that what he says is true.

Thus, to establish states of intention, motive, belief, and so on is often part and parcel of determining what act an agent has performed. But now it is sometimes suggested that precisely because having a motive, for example, is being in the kind of state that may be relevant to the classification of acts, it follows that a motive cannot be the cause of an act it motivates. Melden puts the argument this way:

In any simple causal explanation of one event by reference to another, it is not the identity or the character of the effect that is at issue, but the conditions in which it occurs—how it came to be. Antecedently of the causal explanation given, we know quite well what the event thereby explained is. A causal explanation, in other words, does not give us a further characterization of the event thereby explained.[17]

But since we often get a "further characterization" of a performance from information about, for example, the motive that prompted it, it follows that that motive could not have been the cause.

What is wrong with this argument is that its major premise is false. There is a vast variety of cases in which our classification of an event is determined at least in part by what we know of its etiology. It is, for example, precisely to etiology that we appeal in making a distinction between having a hallucination and seeing a mirage, or between a strep throat and a common cold. So long as there is nothing in logic that would prevent us from classifying effects by their causes, and since there is every precedent for employing such classifications, we cannot deny that motives are causes only on the grounds that it is often the motive for its performance that makes an action the action it is.

A rather more interesting argument, also widely employed by Melden, appeals to the logical independence of cause and effect in order to show that the relation between motives and the actions they motivate cannot be causal. In particular, it is argued that in order to individuate motives, intentions, and so forth we must describe them as motives *for* something— for example, for committing or abstaining from a certain act —or intentions *to do* something—for example, to act or fail to act in a certain way. But the acts in terms of which intentions and motives are specified are precisely those acts that, *ex hypothesis,* citations of the intentions, motives, and so on are supposed to explain causally. This means, in particular, that if motives are causes, then the putative cause of an event is specified in such a way as to include a reference to the event itself. And this, in turn, would appear to violate the Humean stricture that causes must be logically independent of the events they cause.

The argument from Humean strictures is persuasive in that it seems to follow from the remark that causal relations are empirical—that is, not logical—and *that* remark appears, in turn, to be analytic. Yet, if we accept the argument as it is stated, it is unclear what it is supposed to preclude. For example, as Davidson has pointed out,[18] if X caused Y, then "is the cause of Y" is a true description of X. Surely the argument from Humean strictures, whatever it may prove, could not provide grounds for objecting to *this* sort of logical connection between descriptions of the cause and of the effect.

It is, of course, true that if X *is* the cause of Y, then there must be *some* description that is true of X and that is logically independent of the description "Y's cause," and there must be some description that is true of Y and that is logically independent of the description "X's effect." If, however, *that* is what the Humean strictures demand, they are far too weak for Melden's purposes. For example, that demand would be satisfied if the materially sufficient conditions for having a certain motive could be formulated in neurological terms. Indeed, the existence of *any* state of affairs that is associated in a one-to-one fashion with a psychological state, either by a law of nature, or by a true empirical generalization, or by a sheer accident, would permit one to make an identifying reference to that state without referring to the behavior that it is alleged to cause. Suppose, for example, that it happens to be the case that there is a draft in the Tower of London when and only when Smith feels inclined to yawn. Then the feeling Smith has when he feels inclined to yawn could be unequivocally referred to without referring to the yawning by employing some such form of words as "the feeling Smith has whenever the Tower of London is drafty."

Indeed, it appears that, on the present interpretation, the Humean strictures cut no ice whatever; for even when the relation at issue is *not* contingent, there is sure to be some description of X that is logically independent of any description of Y and vice versa. Thus, the relation between three and three can be specified by reference to the contingent relation between the number of weird sisters and the number of planets between Mercury and Earth (inclusive).

It is important to be clear about the limitations of the argument from the logical independence of cause and effect for if it were to be accepted in the strong form in which Melden uses it, it would preclude more than psychology. I have already had occasion to refer to that period in the history of genetics when the best that could be done by way of specifying a gene was to refer to the presumed causal consequences of its presence—that is, when genes were identified as "whatever it is that causes" the blossom to be red or the plant to be tall. This sort of specification of the cause by reference to its effect was harmless—first, because no one doubted that logically independent descriptions of the cause and the effect must eventually be forthcoming and, second, because the data about "directly observable" traits permitted theorists to establish the fact that quite subtle relations of dominance, recessivity, connectedness, and so on must hold between the genes. It was these considerations that made the explanation "Flowers are red because of the presence of red-producing entities" informative, even though the seemingly parallel remark in Molière about morphine and "dormitive power" is not.

This suggests a point that I can only mention but not pursue—namely, that in the interesting cases one can rarely determine whether a form of explanation is "vacuous," "cognitively meaningless," and so on simply by inspection. Rather, one must determine the background of theory and experiment in which the explanation is intended to function, including, perhaps, the scientist's own expectations about the kinds of theories in which the explanation *may* function at some future date. I suspect that it is largely for this reason that the attempt to formalize criteria for empirical significance has invariably proved unsuccessful.

The present point, at any event, is that an important form of scientific inference would be precluded if Humean strictures were to be employed in the way that Melden suggests. Such inferences consist in positing unknown causes for well-known syndromes (genes for recurrent traits, germs for recurrent diseases, etc.). Theory construction involves working out the relations between the entities so specified in a way that extends the range of the phenomena that their postulation explains. In these cases, the entities posited may, in the first instance, be specified by reference to precisely the appearances that they function to save.

This argument works as well against the last grounds that we shall consider for refusing to identify motives and so forth with causes. It has sometimes been suggested that if the connection between psychological states and actions were indeed causal, the assertion that it holds true would need to depend upon the observation of reiterated correlations between them. But since such correlations could be at best "observed" only "in one's own case," one should at best be very uncertain that other people act out of the sorts of motives that are typically and unhesitatingly ascribed to them. In short, if motives are causes, attributions of motives must be inductive inferences—and shaky inductive inferences at that.

Here again, however, the argument depends upon a misapprehension about the sorts of inferences that can lead to the recognition of causal connections. It is obvious that the causal relationship between genes and the traits they produce, or between the red "shift" and the acceleration of stars, was not established by observing that the cause and its effect were constantly correlated. Such observations might possibly be *sufficient* for establishing causal connections, but they are certainly not *necessary*. Nor should it be surprising that this is so. It would, after all, be extraordinary if some among the necessary conditions upon the causal connection served to constrain the ways in which we can discover that it holds true. To put it slightly differently, while it is correct to say that causal connections can obtain only where cause and effect could, in principle, be independently described, it does not by any means follow that the discovery of a causal connection is possible only where the cause and effect have in fact been independently observed.

The argument so far is not intended, of course, to deny that interesting distinctions can be drawn between those propositions that express logical relations and those that express contingent relations. For example, if "If X, then Y" expresses a contingent relation between events of type X and events of type Y, it follows that it is logically possible for no occurrence of type X to have been followed by an occurrence type Y. Now, it might well be maintained that it is logically impossible for no case of intending to do something ever to have been followed by the doing of it. Indeed, it would appear that some such claim would be forced upon anyone who holds that the relation between an intention and the act intended is somehow logical, just as its denial is forced upon anyone who holds that the relation is somehow contingent. Unfortunately, however, even though these entailments of their positions provide a real issue between proponents of the causal account of psychological states and their antagonists, it is no clearer how we are to settle this disagreement than the one that engendered it. If we had a test for logical possibility, we could decide the question of whether intentions are causes by applying it to determine whether "The intention to X caused him to X" is always logically false. Without such a test, it is not evident how we are to decide whether "No performance of type X was ever the consequence of an intention to X" could in principle be contingently true.

There are few controversies in the philosophy of mind that could not be resolved at once if we had a motivated way of drawing the analytic/synthetic distinction. But our inability to draw that distinction is no excuse for begging it. For example, it does no good to argue that since it is unimaginable that no intention should ever have borne fruit, the relation between intentions and actions *must* be logical. For this invites the answer that, in the nontechnical sense of "imagine," one cannot imagine the breakdown of *any* of the relations upon which one's world view is based, contingent or otherwise,[19] while, in the philosophical sense of "imagine," what one can imagine is precisely coextensive with what is logically possible, simply because the notions are interdefined. If intentions were never followed by the intended actions, then all our attempts at psychological explanation, including the most casual ones, would fail together. The fact that this state of affairs is, literally, inconceivable does not show that it is undescribable (viz., that the form of words that describes it is inconsistent), or even that it does not hold true.

It is perhaps unnecessary to add that the situation is not clarified by the suggestion that statements that relate types of intentions to types of actions are "grammatical" (rather than analytic or synthetic), as long as the relevant sense of "grammar" is left undefined. That is to baptize the problem, not to solve it.

One further point. It is possible to think of having the intention to X and X-ing as distinct events—that is, to think of having the intention to X as a type of event that, in principle, might never be followed by X-ing—while admitting that if having the intention to X had never *in fact* been followed by *X*-ing, there would be no point in ever having described that type of event that way. That is, the oblique character of certain descriptions of intentions is compatible with the supposition that having an intention is an event logically distinct from, and causally connected to, acting in a certain way—except that if such causal connections *always* failed, there would presumably be no point in talking of the former events as intentions (rather than as, say, wishes).

Even though Jupiter and Ganymede are distinct bodies, had either failed to exist, certain descriptions would have failed to be true of the other and certain expressions now used to refer to them would then have failed to refer. Thus, it is a fallacy to argue from "Ganymede is a satellite of Jupiter" and "If Jupiter had not existed, it is impossible that satellites of Jupiter should have existed" to "If Jupiter had not existed, Ganymede would not have existed." So too, even assuming the second premise to be true, it is not obviously valid to argue from "Event *E* is having the intention to *X*" and "If *X*-ing never occurred, it is impossible that anyone should have the intention to *X*" to "If *X*-ing never occurred, it is impossible that *E* should have occurred."

We have seen how Melden argues from an examination of the constructs that psychologists and laymen use to explain actions that such constructs could not denote causes. An equally popular argument proceeds the other way around. It is assumed that psychology must be a causal science if it is a science at all. But, it is maintained, causal analysis in the strict sense can only demonstrate the contingency of motions of one kind upon motions of another kind.

To give a causal *explanation* of an event involves at least showing that other conditions being presumed unchanged a change in one variable is a sufficient condition for a change in another. In the mechanical conception of a "cause" it is also demanded that there should be spatial and temporal contiguity between the movements involved.[20]

But, it is argued, if this is the sense of "cause" at issue, the causal explanation of *actions* is impossible, and this for two reasons.

The first has to do with the fact that the movements that can realize a given action may be indefinitely numerous and heterogeneous. (Think how the motions that constitute performances of the action *advancing a bishop three squares* may vary, for example, with the size of the board, or the weight of the pieces. And bishops may also be advanced in "mental" chess.) Since, it is argued:

. . . part of what we mean by "intelligence" is the ability to vary movements relative to a goal in a way which is appropriate to changes in the situation necessary to define it as a goal . . . we could never give a sufficient explanation of an action in causal terms because we could never stipulate the movements which would have to count as dependent variables.[21]

This argument rests on two mistakes, one superficial, the other profound. Superficially, what makes the complexity of the mapping of motions onto actions irrelevant to whether the explanation of the latter could be causal is this: It is clear that, in the sense of causal explanation here at issue, an event has been explained if we can show that sufficient conditions for its occurrence have been satisfied. And it is equally clear that from the fact that many different motions may be associated with the same action, we cannot infer that there is no motion whose occurrence is sufficient for performing the action. But wherever there is such a motion, it is presumably possible to specify the motions upon which *it* is causally contingent. Since by doing so we will have shown that a sufficient condition for the action was satisfied, we will presumably have explained the action in the relevant sense of "explain." It is in precisely this sense that a phonologist might seek to specify those motions of the vocal apparatus that are sufficient for the utterance of, for example, "I have swallowed my nose." It would be a much more ambitious task to provide a characterization of the sets of motions that are *necessary* for the making of such an utterance, but the dubiousness of the latter undertaking surely does not reflect upon the feasibility of the former.

The profound mistake is to suppose that an explanation of a class of interactions requires a *prior* enumeration of the dependent variables. Indeed, in the interesting cases, such as psychology and mechanics, the set of dependent variables is infinite and their enumeration is precisely the function of the theory. Thus the class of mechancial interactions is specified precisely by providing a general, abstract characterization of the necessary and sufficient conditions for a change of trajectory, for example, in terms of such abstract theoretical constructs as force, mass, and momentum. This characterization, together with relevant information about initial states, allows one, in principle, to compute the trajectory of any given physical object. In particular, then, one does *not* proceed by first enumerating the class of possible trajectories and then attempting to pair each one with a condition that is causally sufficient for an object having that trajectory.

Similarly, a psychological theory of actions would presumably attempt to provide general, *abstract* analyses of actions of different sorts. Such analyses would presumably *not* be given in terms of motions, but rather in terms of such theoretical constructs as intentions, goals, and drives. (I do not, of course, intend to suggest that these garden-variety psychological constructs would play any very important role in a sophisticated psychological theory. An important goal of psychological inquiry is the discovery of *new kinds of mental events*. [Cf. Freud on "repression," Hull on "retroactive inhibition," Lorenz on "imprinting," and so on.]) It would be hoped that sufficient information about initial states, *together with a viable theory of actions,* would, in principle, permit the theorist to compute the pattern of motions that will realize a given action on a given occasion. The fact that under different initial conditions the same action may be realized as a different pattern of motions is irrelevant to the feasibility of this goal, just as the fact that under different initial conditions the same interaction of forces determines different trajectories is irrelevant to the feasibility of constructing a theory of mechanics.

The argument just discussed seems plausible only because it is easily confused with a much more forceful one. Consider the difference between *uttering* "I have swallowed my nose" and *asserting* it. It is at least arguable that the first is an action that might conceivably be performed by someone who had no knowledge of English—for example, by someone who uttered the sentence during the course of uttering sounds at random. But, clearly, asserting that one has swallowed one's nose by using that combination of words can be done, so to speak, only against the background of a knowledge of English. Similarly, in one sense of "Move the bishop," one can do so simply by making an appropriate gesture. But moving the bishop counts as making a move only when the rules of the game are in force.

The point of this argument is that however intimately a certain motion may be associated with a corresponding action, there are many cases when, by definition, the occurrence of the motion counts as a performance of the action only under conditions that cannot be specified solely by reference to further motions. These are cases not of there being *many* motions corresponding to a given action, but of there being

no motion whose performance is sufficient for the performance of the action. Now, insofar as psychological explanations
account only for motions, such explanations must, if this
argument is correct, fall short of accounting for actions.

The first thing to observe about this argument is that
it depends upon certain necessary truths about actions, and
hence is not an argument particularly about human behavior
or psychological explanation (unless one holds it to be
analytic that only persons, or only organisms, can perform
actions). Consider, for example, a self-correcting clock. At
a certain point the minute hand of such a clock is observed
to move 15 degrees. Upon inquiry we may be told *either*
that it did so because the gears and pulleys did such and such
or that it jumped because it was running five minutes slow
and it always corrects itself at noon. The latter explanation
introduces the sort of background of motives, rules, conventions, intentions, and so on that are characteristically
operative in the ascription of actions to persons. It is thus
refractory to mechanistic translation in precisely the same
way as statements about some actions of persons are (though
no one would argue from this that the clock is therefore not
a mechanism).

Such considerations suggest that whatever else one says
about the implications of the present analysis of actions,
their relevance to the libertarian controversies in which they
often figure is dubious. They do not, however, show that the
argument against the possibility of causal explanations of
actions is fallacious. Indeed, it is clearly not. That is, if by
hypothesis causal explanations explain only motions, and
if by hypothesis some actions are logically distinct from motions, then, clearly, causal explanations cannot explain those
latter actions.

But though the argument is sound (barring certain questions that may be raised about the notion of causal explanation at issue) it is in a certain sense uninteresting. For suppose it turned out to be a sufficient condition for an organism to perform a certain action that it performed some motion while it was in a certain state—for example, it might be supposed that certain motions count as certain actions only when they are performed with a certain motive or in the light of certain rules or on account of certain interests, and so forth. Since it is granted that any *motion* of an organism could, in principle, be causally explained, the problem of the explicability of these *actions* would reduce to the question whether sufficient conditions for the relevant state could be specified in an appropriate vocabulary. A vocabulary is "appropriate" in the present sense if its terms denote only such entities as are clearly capable of figuring in causal transactions. Hence it would be a sufficient condition for the causal explanation of an action that:

1. the action can be analyzed as a motion that is performed by an organism in a certain state, and
2. sufficient causal conditions for being in that state can be formulated; for example, in physiological terms.

This is to say, in effect, that whether actions whose definition requires reference to the motives, reasons, or intentions of the agent can be causally explained depends on whether physiologically sufficient conditions for having motives, reasons, and intentions can be specified.

Note that since our current account of causal explanations requires only that we demonstrate that a certain action occurs whenever specified conditions are satisfied, we are *not* required to suppose that motives, reasons, and so forth must be *identified* with physiological states in order for the causal explanation of actions to be possible. We need only suppose that the occurrence of such states is empirically sufficient for having motives, reasons, and so on and that the actions in question can be analyzed as motions that the organism performs for the relevant reasons, or with the relevant intentions. If it be said that these are weak conditions to place upon the causal explanation of behavior, it must be replied that the view that causal explanation consists in exhibiting the contingency of motions on motions is itself utterly unsatisfactory. If I explain Smith's behavior by reference to the alcohol he drank, the explanation is causal in any sense to which the most mechanistic psychologist might aspire. But neither the cause nor the effect alluded to can happily be construed as a motion.

In short, the fact that some actions cannot be identified with motions does not *by itself* show that the causal explanation of those actions is impossible. For it leaves open the possibility that they may be identifiable with motions performed in states for which sufficient conditions can be formulated in appropriate causal language. The argument does show, however, that actions cannot, in principle, be provided with causal *psychological* explanations in certain cases in which the background required for performances of the action constrains states of the environment rather than states of the organism. What must legally be the case for a certain motion to count as signing a deed, for example, cannot be stated in terms of either the states *or* the motions of the signer. (Compare what must be the case for an agent to perform an action that *he takes* to be the signing of a deed.) If, then, psychology is a causal science, and if causes cause only motions, such actions as signing a deed do not fall within its competence—namely, for the trivial reason that a science that formulated causal conditions for the existence of a legal system would ipso facto not be considered a branch of psychology. Hence some of the states for which sufficient conditions would need to be provided to causally explain the signing of a deed are not *psychological* states.

It should be fairly clear that nothing more than a terminological question is involved here; a terminological stipulation would therefore appear to be the appropriate answer to the question. If one wishes to preserve the generality of psychological explanation from this sort of criticism without abandoning one's hope of a causal psychology, one might say that signing a deed is not a bit of behavior in any sense of that term that interests a psychologist. (Saying that "signing a deed" is not a description of behavior would then be akin to saying that "spending more than you can afford" is from the physicist's point of view, not a description of a physical event.) I think that this is an intuitively plausible suggestion. One would not, for example, attempt to refute the claim that a certain machine is capable of simulating human behavior by pointing out that signing deeds is not one of the acts in its repertoire. One would be satisfied if the machine were capable of producing behavior that, given the current legal background, would count as signing a deed if it were performed by a person. (There is, in fact, some point to adopting a usage according to which it is analytic that behavior, in the technical sense, includes precisely that part of what an organism does that it makes logical sense to try to simulate.)

In short, the present argument returns us to a conclusion at which we had previously arrived. Nothing so far shows that psychology may not be general, in whatever sense that term can be applied to the other sciences, or that the psychologist may not reasonably seek to provide explanations of a type that would be acceptable in the other sciences. In particular, nothing shows that a causal explanation may not be provided for each behavior under some description. On the other hand, since how we count behaviors and what is available as a description depends in part on what conceptual equipment our theories provide, whether and in what respects psychological explanations are general are questions that cannot be answered prior to the development of reasonably adequate psychological theories.[22]

 # TWO

Behaviorism and Mentalism

If there is a received view about psychological explanation among Anglo-American philosophers and experimental psychologists, it is surely that one or another form of behaviorism is true. At first glance this is surprising, since behaviorism by no means recommends itself on grounds of its inherent plausibility. On the contrary, its adherents are forever warning us to distrust our intuitions, which, they say, have been corrupted by Cartesianism or by misunderstandings of ordinary language or by both. It is only through prolonged and sophisticated philosophical therapy, according to this view, that these influences can be mitigated and an innocent ear regained.

The wide acceptance of behaviorism among philosophers is, nevertheless, far from inexplicable. In the first place, as we shall presently see, the logical character of behaviorism is such as to render it morally incompatible with dualism and logically incompatible with skepticism, and both dualism and skepticism are doctrines that most philosophers today prefer not to espouse. Second, the arguments in favor of behaviorism derive from extremely persuasive empiricistic accounts of language, of knowledge and of the nature of scientific theories. These accounts are mutually supportive, so that behaviorism may be defended by appeal to what amounts to a general system of empiricist philosophy, thereby inheriting its plausibility from the coherence and force of that system.

To attack behaviorism with any hope of success therefore requires at least a cursory examination of relevant aspects of that entire system. In particular, it must be determined whether the epistemological, linguistic, and methodological views from which behaviorism draws its support are themselves plausible. This chapter will undertake to make such an examination. I shall try to sort out the different kinds of arguments for behaviorism in a way in which its defenders have not always bothered to do. I shall then try to show that the principles to which these arguments appeal are quite unsatisfactory.

It is difficult for a discussion of behaviorism to simultaneously avoid terminological confusion and stipulative definition, for many philosophers whose views it would seem natural to call behavioristic are apparently offended by the term. Thus, whereas psychologists are inclined to use "behaviorism" to cover a wide variety of S-R and mediational theories, a practice has developed in the philosophical literature of using the word only to refer to what might more properly be called "radical behaviorism"—that is, to the view that mental words are literally definable in behavioral terms. Moreover, this sort of terminological trouble is by no means specific to the use of "behaviorism." It is often far from clear precisely what philosophers and psychologists have in mind when they are talking about such related doctrines as mentalism, dualism, skepticism, and materialism. I therefore propose to start by attempting to impose at least a rough taxonomy upon the major options in the field, one that will permit a preliminary sketch of the logical relations among these options.

Versions of Behaviorism

To begin with, I shall use "behaviorism" liberally because I think that the sorts of considerations to be raised here hold equally for both the strict and the loose forms of the doctrine. To qualify as a behaviorist in the broad sense of that term that I shall employ, one need only believe that the following proposition expresses a necessary truth: For each mental predicate that can be employed in a psychological explanation, there must be at least one description of behavior to which it bears a logical connection. I shall henceforth refer to this proposition as P. (We are not, of course, concerned with connections that are mediated by formal logic. Thus it is of no interest to the present argument that, if P is a true proposition containing a mental predicate, it implies PvQ, where Q may contain some behavioral predicates.)

P is worth investigating because the claim that it is necessarily true is common to a number of otherwise quite different formulations of behaviorism—that is, if *any* of these formulations is true, then P is true necessarily. Thus, I take it that the necessity of P is entailed by (but does not entail) the familiar philosophical doctrines associated with such slogans as: mental events require behavioral criteria; intervening variables in psychological explanations must be tied to observables "at both ends"; theoretical terms in psychological explanations must, in principle, be eliminable in favor of (definable by) terms that designate observables; psychological theories are smooth projections of observed correlations between the input and output states of organisms; there exists a "grammatical" connection between each mental predicate and some behavioral predicates.

All the key terms in P need explication: "mental predicate," "description of behavior," "logical connection." The different ways of understanding these terms lead to correspondingly different versions of behaviorism.

For example, to interpret the demand for a logical connection between mental and behavioral predicates as requiring that the former be definable in terms of the latter is to espouse the doctrine that I referred to above as "radical behaviorism." One obtains a weaker form of behaviorism by interpreting the requirement of logical connection as demanding only that logically necessary and sufficient conditions for the application of mental predicates be specifiable in behavioral terms, or else that either logically sufficient conditions should be so specifiable or that logically necessary conditions should be. Moreover, a very considerable part of the recent literature on the philosophy of mind has suggested that there may be some sense of "logical connection" such that two propositions may be so connected even though neither of them specifies either a necessary or a sufficient condition for the truth of the other. A number of such accounts of the alleged connection between mental and behavioral ascriptions will be reviewed in this chapter. Suffice it to remark here that while each view of the nature of logical connections yields a corresponding interpretation of P (and hence a corresponding form of behaviorism), the family resemblances between all such doctrines is patent.

Since behaviorists differ about the nature of the alleged logical connection between mental and behavioral ascriptions, it would be misleading to use the traditional language of implication and entailment to describe what is common to their views. I shall therefore formulate the generic behaviorist position as asserting *either* that each mental ascription "logically implicates" some behavioral descriptions, *or* that some behavioral descriptions logically implicate mental ascriptions, *or* both. It will be understood that "logically implicate" is a cover term for any of the various types of logical relation that may be said to hold between behavioral and mental language. Moreover, I shall often use such terms as "description," "ascription," "proposition," and "assertion" interchangeably, since, for present purposes, it is indifferent whether the behaviorist maintains that the relevant connections hold between mental terms, or between sentences containing mental terms, or between the uses to which such sentences may be put, etc.

Just as different versions of behaviorism are generated by different interpretations of "logical connection," so the details of a behaviorist's position will reflect his understanding of the notion of "behavioral description." It is evident that the behaviorist's position will be most defensible (and least interesting) if he permits as behavioral descriptions such locutions as "eating hungrily," "writhing in agony," or "smiling happily," for it is hardly to be doubted that "writhing in agony" is logically related to "being in agony." Writhe as one may, one is patently not writhing in agony unless it is agony that is causing one to writhe. Hence, if "writhing in agony" counts as a description of behavior, there is ipso facto at least one case of a logical connection between a behavioral description and a mental predicate.

The difficulty with this sort of defense of behaviorism is that the theory that is being defended has none of the properties that lend the stronger versions of behaviorism their appeal. For example, psychologists and philosophers of science who espouse behaviorism often do so because they are impressed by the need to eliminate from the "observation base" of a psychological theory—that is, from the vocabulary in which its predictions are couched—any terms whose application requires "interpretation" of the confirming phenomena. It must, they argue, be possible to determine by purely observational procedures whether or not a prediction of the theory has been verified, since to use theoretical constructs in describing those phenomena upon which the confirmation of the theory depends is held to be circular. To describe behavior in such terms as "writhing in agony" presumably requires interpreting the observed states and movements of an organism by reference to certain standards. Hence, according to the stricter forms of behaviorism, "writhing in agony" and, in general, its logical kin must be eliminated from reports of the observations upon which the truth of psychological theories is based.

A central principle of empiricist epistemology has been to require the isolation of "inductive risk" at some level of theory construction that is formally distinguishable from the level at which the data statements are articulated, thus bestowing upon the latter a unique privilege of unrevisability and hence a unique type of cognitive certainty. The application of this principle in the case of psychology requires a theoretically neutral language for the description of the primary psychological data; that is, of behavior. It is for this reason that a defense of behaviorism that makes "behavior" itself a theoretical term is only in a Pickwickian sense a defense of *behaviorism*. If the point of behaviorism is to be preserved, it must be taken as analytic that whether and how an organism is behaving are questions to be settled by observation, in the sense of that term in which what is observed is ipso facto not inferred.[1]

But while it is clear that certain locutions must be denied the status of descriptions of behavior if behaviorism is to be worth discussing, a considerable number of positions are left open as answers to the question of what sorts of descriptions *are* to count as behavioral—for example, descriptions of the states of the musculature of an organism, or of its movements, or of its sequence of postures. As with interpretations of "logical connection," the possibilities are limited only by the ingenuity of the behaviorist and by the requirement that he take no liberties that would lead to the trivializing of his position. Once again, however, the differences among the varieties of behaviorism that exploitation of the various possibilities for interpreting "behavioral description" may lead to will concern us less than their similarities will.

Mentalism and Behaviorism

Having fixed a technical meaning for "behaviorism," I now need a term of art for its denial. I shall adopt "mentalism" for that purpose. A mentalist is, then, simply someone who denies "necessarily *P*."

These terminological stipulations have some slightly eccentric consequences that had better be made explicit. In the first place, as I am using the two words, the distinction between mentalism and behaviorism is both exclusive and exhaustive. You must be either a mentalist or a behaviorist because you must believe of "necessarily *P*" either that it is true or that it is false. Second, I am using "mentalism" in a way that requires distinguishing between mentalism and dualism, and that distinction is not always made in the philosophical literature. By "dualism" I mean the doctrine that mental and behavioral predicates apply to subjects of essentially different logical types—that is, that mental predicates designate states of minds and that minds are substances of a kind that are irreducibly different from the bodies to which behavioral predicates apply. Roughly, a dualist is someone who maintains both that minds and bodies are things and also that they are things *of different kinds.*

It is easy to confuse mentalism with dualism since a dualist is likely to be a mentalist as well. That is, if you hold that behavioral predicates apply to a kind of subject that is logically different from the kind of subject to which mental predicates apply, you will probably not hold as well that there are logical connections between predicates of the two kinds. This is not simply a matter of taste. It is clear that embracing dualism logically precludes holding that certain sorts of logical connections could obtain between mental and behavioral predicates. Dualism is logically incompatible with certain varieties of behaviorism.

It is patent, for example, that one cannot hold that mental and behavioral predicates apply to logically different sorts of subjects and at the same time hold that the former are definable in terms of the latter; not, at least, on the assumption that definition requires intersubstitutability of definiens and definiendum. Analogously, one cannot be a dualist and also hold that the truth of behavioral ascriptions provides logically sufficient conditions for the truth of mental ascriptions; for to say that minds and bodies are different types of substances is to say at least that the existence of either is logically independent of the existence of the other (in the way in which the existence of bachelors is *not* logically independent of the existence of male unmarried persons). But this condition would be violated if it were sometimes possible to deduce the truth of mental ascriptions from the truth of behavioral ascriptions, or vice versa.

Although all dualists are likely to be mentalists, the converse is by no means true. To maintain that statements about minds and statements about behavior are logically independent is fully compatible with maintaining that mental and behavioral predicates apply to substances of the same kind

—for example, either to persons or to physical objects. We thus arrive at a third respect in which the terminology adopted here differs from what is traditional in the philosophical literature. Since it is clear that the doctrine that "necessarily *P*" is false is fully compatible with any variety of monism, it follows, in particular, that mentalism as here defined is compatible with materialism as traditionally defined. In particular, it is compatible with the doctrine that mind states and brain states are contingently identical.

Though arid, terminological points of the sort we have been surveying are not unimportant. For example, accepting the distinction between behaviorism, mentalism, and dualism enables us to understand some of the factors that have determined the course of much recent theorizing in the philosophy of mind.

Mentalism and Dualism

We saw above that mentalism is a necessary concomitant of at least some varieties of dualism, and that it is thus not surprising that the distinction between these doctrines has frequently been ignored. The consequence of this confusion is that analytic philosophers have often sought to show that dualism is untenable, *not* by attacking the two-substance theory, but rather by providing arguments against mentalism. This is clearly the pattern of argument in Ryle's *Concept of Mind,*[2] where what Ryle puts forward as an attack upon the "Cartesian Myth" (i.e., upon the theory that minds and bodies are different kinds of substances) is a putative demonstration that some psychological predicates can be analyzed as designating dispositions to produce certain kinds of behavior. This attack is, very likely, misdirected against Descartes, who would presumably have replied that even if psychological terms denote dispositions to behave in certain ways, a causally necessary condition for being so disposed is being in the relevant mental state. (It is worth remembering that one reason for Descartes' dualism was his belief that appeals to mental events must figure in causal explanations of behavior.) On the other hand, if Ryle's arguments were sound, they would be incompatible with *mentalism,* since they purport to show that behavioral entailments enter into the analysis of mental terms.

The Concept of Mind is by no means the only influential work in analytic philosophy in which arguments that are logically relevant to mentalism are put forth as though they were arguments against dualism. For example, it seems fairly obvious that part of the intent of the psychological sections of Wittgenstein's *Philosophical Investigations*[3] is to present an array of arguments designed to establish that the existence of behavioral criteria is logically prerequisite to the use of mental terms, at least in certain of their employments. It is along these lines that Wittgenstein proposes to demonstrate the incoherence of the dualistic view that mental terms designate some sort of internal objects. To cite still another example, the attack upon dualism in Strawson's *Individuals*[4] depends upon his showing that it is a defining characteristic of *P* (mental) predicates that the satisfaction of behavioral criteria should be logically sufficient for their second-person applications.

While it is clear that a preferred line of argument against dualism has often been to seek to establish a logical connection between behavioral and mental ascriptions, it is less clear that there has been a wide realization of the possibility that dualism and behaviorism may *both* be false. That is, philosophers who have wanted to banish the ghost from the machine have usually sought to do so by showing that truths about behavior can sometimes, and in some sense, logically implicate truths about mental states. In so doing, they have rather strongly suggested that the exorcism can be carried through *only* if such a logical connection can be made out. If this description of the state of the literature is correct, it is clear that the diagnosis must be that the compulsion these philosophers have felt to demonstrate behaviorism, on pain of otherwise falling into dualism, has arisen out of a failure to distinguish the latter from mentalism. Once that distinction has been drawn, once it has been made clear that the choice between dualism and behaviorism is not exhaustive, a major motivation for the defense of behaviorism is removed: we are not required to be behaviorists simply in order to avoid being dualists.[5]

Mentalism and Materialism

In order to show that there are arguments against dualism that are logically independent of the truth of behaviorism, it is necessary only to review such familiar considerations as the following: It is tautological that, if there are mental events of the sort that the dualist has in mind, their postulation either is or is not required for the causal explanation of some nonmental (e.g., behavioral) events. On the former contingency, it is difficult to understand why we should not think of the putatively mental events as merely a special kind of physical events, since it is presumably a sufficient condition for something to be a physical event that it be implicated in causal transactions. If, on the other hand, reference to the alleged mental events is *not* required in order to explain the causation of nonmental events, it is difficult to see how mental events are to escape Occam's razor. For there is then, *ex hypothesis,* no datum for whose causal explanation they are required. In short, it seems that the dualist must be committed either to interactionism or to parallelism. But the former appears to fail on grounds of incoherence; the latter, on grounds of unnecessary complexity.

It should be emphasized that arguments of this sort, whatever their merits may be, do *not* hold against mentalism. The compatibility of mentalism with materialism permits a mentalist to agree that there may be some behavioral events in whose causal explanation mental events figure—for example, because the behavior is the effect of the neurological causes with which, on the materialist's account, mental events are to be identified. But it by no means follows from this that, if materialism were true, considerations of simplicity would require the elimination of mental language from psychological theories. Even on the view that mind states and brain states are in fact identical, the propositions that assert such identities are surely only contingent. Hence, on the assumption that materialism is correct, it would still be the case that there are some true, contingent propositions that cannot be formulated unless mental language is employed: namely, all the propositions that assert of specified mental states that they are identical with specified physiological states.[6]

Behaviorism and Skepticism

We have thus far pursued a rather sketchy analysis of some of the logical relations among mentalism, behaviorism, dualism, and materialism. We have seen that one possible way of arguing against dualism is to establish some form of behaviorism, and that, in point of historical fact, a major motivation for adopting behaviorism has been the mistaken supposition that it provides the only viable line of argument against dualism.

Dualism is, however, but one of the two skeletons in the

behaviorist's closet. In order to understand this, one must take note of the fact that, of the various views of psychological constructs that we have mentioned so far, only behaviorism is logically incompatible with the truth of certain sorts of skeptical assertions about the reality of other minds and about the truth of our knowledge claims concerning other minds.

Like behaviorism, skepticism is best understood as a family of related doctrines, all of them susceptible to a family of related counterarguments. Of a skeptic who maintains that we can never have reasons for supposing that mental predicates apply to persons other than ourselves, it would be pertinent to inquire into what his concept is of "having a reason." Of a skeptic who maintains that we can never properly claim to know that any minds other than our own exist, it would be pertinent to inquire into his use of "know." Of a skeptic who holds that we can never arrive at better than probable knowledge of the existence or operations of other minds, it would be pertinent to inquire whether "probable" has not in this context lost that logical possibility of providing a contrast with "certain" that is presumably characteristic of its proper employment outside philosophy.

I want to distinguish all such varieties of skepticism from an extremely modest position that I shall call "minimal skepticism." Minimal skepticism seems to me to be interesting in two respects. In the first place, it formulates an important insight that underlies classical skepticism in something like the way in which the claim that statements about the past never entail statements about the future underlies the classical skeptical arguments about induction. Second, its very modesty renders it proof against the sort of antiskeptical arguments alluded to in the preceding paragraph.

I shall say that someone is a minimal skeptic if he maintains that there are cases in which we can not know with logical certainty what mental state someone is in, and then defends that claim by arguing that there are some statements about minds whose truth is not logically implicated by any statements about interpersonally observables. That is to say, minimal skepticism rests upon the premise that there are some statements about minds, the truth of which is logically independent of the truth of any statement about behavior. Minimal skepticism is thus an attenuated version of the conventional skepticism that maintains that we can never be logically certain that mental ascriptions hold because *no* mental ascription is ever logically implicated by any behavioral ascription.

It should be noted that the question of whether minimal skepticism is true is related to one of the questions that we discussed in Chapter I. Since it is logically possible for any causal explanation to be false, a sufficient condition would be made out for the truth of minimal skepticism if it could be shown that mental states characteristically cause the behaviors they are invoked to explain. Someone who claims that psychological terms denote causes of behavior is thus ipso facto committed to minimal skepticism.

But that is not the only way in which this bundle of problems is tied together. For it must be apparent that minimal skepticism is one immediate consequence of the denial of behaviorism. What behaviorism asserts and mentalism denies is that there must be logical connections between any mental ascriptions and some behavioral ascriptions. If we assume with the mentalist that, for at least some predicates, no such connection need obtain, and if we agree to the usage according to which we "know with logical certainty" that someone is in such and such a mental state *only* when the fact that he is in that state is logically implicated by facts about his behavior, it follows immediately that there must be conceivable cases in which we could not know with logical certainty what mental state someone is in.

The skeptic's argument, then, is that if mentalism is true, the inference from behavioral to mental ascriptions is always contingent in the case of at least some mental terms. But where the inference is contingent, it is logically fallible.

Epistemological Arguments for Behaviorism

Here, then, is the point at which the epistemological arguments for behaviorism make their entrance. For it is easy enough to make out a case that the skeptical consequences of the acceptance of mentalism are awkward consequences. Other people's moods, sensations, feelings, and so forth are surely just the sorts of things of which we often and unhesitatingly claim to be certain. Must there not, then, be something seriously in error in a view of mental ascriptions that would require us to abandon all such claims? In short, if mentalism leads in only one step to the impossibility of our being certain about the truth of our claims regarding other minds, there must surely be something wrong with mentalism.

Conversely, it would appear to be a very powerful argument in favor of adopting some variety of behaviorism that if P is necessarily true, it is possible to account for the fact that we *are* sometimes sure of the correctness of our knowledge claims about other minds. On the behaviorists' view, it is indeed possible—in principle at least—that on some occasions and in some sense of "logical," the application of any mental term may be warranted by a logical inference from behavior. Hence, on the assumption that P is necessary, it is part of the logic of mental terms that it is possible in principle for us sometimes to be certain that those terms are correctly applied to persons other than ourselves.

Minimal skepticism (and hence mentalism) is committed to the view that our knowledge of the mental states of others amounts to something less (or rather, something other) than logical certainty. Thus the considerations indicated above would tell against the minimal skeptic if there were any grounds for holding that the sort of certainty that we often have about the mental state of someone whose behavior we have observed is in fact correctly described as logical certainty. But it is very far from clear what sort of grounds these could be.

The problem is that we need, but do not have, a way of distinguishing between logical certainty and what might be called moral certainty. For it is perfectly evident that there are many contingent propositions whose denial we would properly characterize as absurd. That is, there are many propositions that it would be absurd to deny, even though our grounds for believing them are not logically sufficient, in even the most inflationary sense of "logical." My present certainty that New York City is in New York State is, I suppose, an example of this kind. I have no evidence that would logically implicate the truth of that proposition, and the proposition is clearly contingent (Kansas City is in Missouri). Yet, on the basis of what I do know, it would be linguistically correct for me to stigmatize as preposterous the claim that New York City is *not* in New York State. This is not very puzzling; it is simply a fact about English that a proposition need not be necessary in order for its denial properly to be described as absurd.

There are, then, some contingent propositions about which we can correctly claim to be certain. Among these are those propositions for which we have conclusive evidence— but conclusive evidence need not (perhaps cannot) entail the proposition for which it *is* evidence. Again, there are a number of cases in which claims to be certain about contingent propositions are credited not on the basis of evidence, but rather because the person who makes the claim is known to be in a position to make claims of that sort. What one says about one's name, one's marital status, one's date of birth, and so forth has that sort of privilege. One's prima facie right to pronounce upon such matters would be challenged only in very unusual circumstances: suspicion of pathology, fraud, bigamy, and so on. Barring such circumstances, if you are asked why you are so certain about your name, the right answer is not to cite your evidence but simply to remind the inquirer that it is *your* name, after all.

A serious inquiry into the epistemology of our ordinary language would presumably need to distinguish these (and other) cases from the ones that form the stock examples in the texts—for example, from being certain that the sun will rise tomorrow, or from being certain that the next bachelor one encounters will be unmarried. Such an inquiry would likely exhibit a complex of bases to which we can appeal when our claim to be certain about a proposition is questioned, as well as a correspondingly elaborate vocabulary for criticizing claims that propositions that we are certain about are false. In this latter arsenal, "logically incoherent" is only one weapon, along with "preposterous," "unimaginable," "absurd," "not worth considering," and so on. Some of the plausibility of what is sometimes called "logical behaviorism" derives from the mistake of supposing that incoherence is the only charge that can be leveled against the saying of something silly.

The point of these remarks is that it is a mistake to argue from "*S* is certain" or from "The denial of *S* is absurd" to "*S* is necessary" or to "*S* is true a priori." It is, moreover, a serious mistake in that it very often leads philosophers to adopt implausible theories (typically, theories of language or of knowledge) in order to account for the putative necessity of some of the propositions they are certain about. Almost always, when a philosopher invokes the principles of Transcendental Logic (or, recently, of "Depth Grammar" or "Informal Logic"), he is about to parade in the trappings of necessity some certainty that formal logic declines to guarantee.[7]

In short, then, the minimal skeptic and his mentalist ally need not admit that, because we are often certain what mental state someone is in when we have observed his behavior, there must therefore be a logical connection between behavioral and mental ascriptions. The dilemma that the behaviorist poses for the skeptic—either there is a logical connection between mental and behavioral predicates, or else our certainty about some mental ascriptions is inexplicable—may properly be said to rest upon an insufficiently subtle appreciation of the varied ways in which such words as "certain" work.

We have seen that the behaviorist fails to make out a satisfactory case for the claim that the necessity of P is a precondition for the possibility of being certain about mental ascriptions: not all cases of certainty depend upon appeals to a priori truths, and nothing so far has shown that we ever have, in fact, anything more than moral certainty about the truth of mental ascriptions. Parallel arguments suggest that the necessity of P may be independent as well of the proper working of mental language in a number of other cases.

For example, the absence of logical connections between statements about behavior and statements about minds is compatible with the possibility that the truth of statements of one sort should provide reasons (good, adequate, etc.) for believing statements of the other sort. Indeed, one could perfectly well maintain that there are necessary statements of the form "That Q is a reason for maintaining that R," where Q is an ascription of behavior and R is a mental ascription, and still hold that there is no logical connection between Q

and *R tout court*. Such a view would amount to claiming that
there is a logical inference from certain behavioral ascriptions
to assertions of the form "There is every reason for maintaining *R*" or to "Assertions that *R* are justified"—which is fully
compatible with there being no logical inference from such
ascriptions to *R*.

There is every reason for maintaining that a child who
exhibits spots and is feverish, photophobic, and so on has
measles. And it might even be plausibly maintained that
that statement is necessarily true, since the symptoms mentioned are surely more or less characteristic of the measles
syndrome, and it is analytic that a good reason for saying
that someone has ϕ is that he exhibits the ϕ syndrome. There
is, however, no logical inference from exhibiting the syndrome
to actually having measles. Rather, different diseases may
have closely similar syndromes—which is what makes dif-
ferential diagnosis an art. In short, there can be no logical
inference from the syndrome to the disease because what is
definitive of measles is that certain symptoms are exhibited
with a certain etiology, and the inference from an effect to
its cause, however well warranted (by theory or induction,
or by both), must surely be contingent.

But if this account is correct, it is unclear what prevents
the mentalist from maintaining, for example, both that it is
analytic that if someone exhibits a certain sort of behavior,
there is reason for supposing that he is in pain ("That's precisely the sort of thing we *call* a reason for supposing that
someone is in pain") *and* that inferences from the behavior
to the pain are all contingent—possibly because the relevant
relations between pain and pain behavior are all causal.

It appears that one must resist the temptation to hold
that wherever "*P* is a reason for *Q*" is analytic, inferences
from *P* to *Q* are therefore quasi-logical. It is presumably

analytic that the fact that all the swans one has observed are white is a reason for believing that all swans are white. But the inference from the proposition about what has been observed to the lawlike proposition is a classic case of inductive extrapolation, and surely if any inferences ever fail to be quasi-logical, inductive inferences do.

The truth of behaviorism thus appears to be independent both of the possibility of reasoning about the application of mental predicates and of the possibility of sometimes being certain that one has reasoned correctly. It should be noted next that behaviorism may be false, even though some statements of the form "If Q, then *ceteris paribus R*" are necessary, where Q is a purely behavioral description and R is a mental ascription. (I assume that the *ceteris paribus* clause is understood to be equivalent to a [perhaps infinite] disjunction of statements about the "background conditions" in which the behavior described by Q occurs, so that the *ceteris paribus* clause in the statement "If someone is flushed, talks loudly, stamps his foot, strikes out, etc., then, *ceteris paribus,* he is angry" means something like "assuming that he is not acting a part, or having a fit, or attempting to deceive, etc.")

It seems evident that to establish a nontrivial connection between the behavioral terms in Q and the mental terms in R, it is necessary to show that no mental terms appear ineliminably in the list of background conditions of which the *ceteris paribus* clause is an abbreviation. For it is surely not enough for the behaviorist to show that each mental predicate is logically connected to some list of terms in which *both* mental and behavioral terms appear. No one, for example, denies that the truth of a mental ascription may be entailed by the truth of a conjunction of a behavioral description with such typically mental statements as "There was no intention to deceive," or "He was not pretending." For, on the mentalist's view, the force of such addenda would be to assert that the subject really *is* in the mental state his behavior makes him appear to be in. And, of course, "*X* is angry" is entailed by "*X* is behaving in a way that makes it appear that he is angry, and the appearances are not misleading."

The question that is relevant to the truth of behaviorism is not whether "If *Q*, then *ceteris paribus R*" is sometimes necessary under the relevant substitutions for *Q* and *R*. It is rather whether it still remains necessary after we have eliminated all mentalistic language in our unpacking of the *ceteris paribus* clause. So far as I know, there is nowhere in the philosophical literature a serious attempt to show that the answer to that question is affirmative. If, however, the occurrence of mental terms is *not* eliminable from the specifications for normalcy conditions, it seems clear that logical connections between behavioral language and mental language of the sort that *ceteris paribus* clauses are capable of mediating are too weak to be of service to the behaviorist.

Finally, it is sometimes said that there is at least *this* much grammatical connection between pain behavior and pain: if someone is exhibiting what is clearly pain behavior, then the burden of proof is upon anyone who denies that he is in pain; that is, there is at least a prima facie inference from pain behavior to pain so that, barring specific reasons to the contrary, reference to pain behavior is adequate to justify pain ascription.

Once again, however, the truth of this contention is compatible with the possibility that there is no logical connection between sensation language and behavioral language so that the soundness of prima facie arguments from pain behavior to pain proves nothing that is useful to the behaviorist. Proving that an animal has a backbone is prima facie adequate to prove that it has a heart. Hence, if I have found the one, the burden of proof is on you if you choose to deny that I will find the other. For all that, no one holds that "All vertebrates have hearts" expresses a necessary truth.

Mental Terms and Behavioral Dispositions

One further point needs to be made before we bring to an end our discussion of epistemological arguments that have been alleged in favor of behaviorism. Just as the truth of mentalism is compatible with the necessity of certain inferences (from behavior to mental states) that are mediated by *ceteris paribus* clauses, so is it also compatible with the possibility that there is a logical connection between certain mental terms and terms that denote (or whose applicability entails) dispositions to produce behavior. For example, it is fully compatible with the truth of mentalism that such statements as "If X causes pain to Y, then Y is disposed to avoid X" should be necessary. The necessity of such connections between mental and dispositional terms would supply a logical connection between mental ascriptions and behavioral ascriptions *tout court,* only if it could be shown: (1) that some descriptions of behavior would logically implicate that the relevant dispositional holds, or (2) that the conditions under which the disposition is correctly said to be realized can be specified in purely behavioral language—that is, without the use of such mental notions as "intentionally," "on purpose," or "knowing what he was doing."

1. That no purely behavioral description could logically implicate the sorts of dispositionals that are entailed by certain mental ascriptions is suggested by the following considerations. The context "Y is disposed to ———" is intensional for descriptions of behavior when Y ranges over persons. That is, one usually determines what someone was disposed to do by ascertaining the intentions with which he did what-

ever he was observed to do; "intending to do" and "doing" are very often not the same. This means, however, that it is at best not obvious that the truth of such statements as "*Y* is disposed to avoid *X*" could be logically implicated by any description of the behavior of *Y* that did not also mention *Y*'s mental state: what *Y* believed, intended, hoped, wished, and so on. In particular, it would certainly not be implicated by the truth of "*Y* avoided *X*," insofar as that statement is supposed to be a description of *Y*'s behavior.

2. But it is also doubtful that the conditions under which dispositionals that are logically connected to mental terms are realized can be specified in purely behavioral terms. It is characteristic of certain mental ascriptions that they entail dispositions to behave in certain ways *for certain ends, with certain intentions,* and so on. But it is by no means evident that the behavior that realizes such dispositionals could be specified without these mentalistic addenda, or that the addenda could themselves be provided with analyses in purely behavioral language. If having an itch is logically connected to *any* disposition, it is to a disposition to scratch *with an eye toward relieving an annoying sensation* (random scratching won't do). But this connection is surely of no use to the behaviorist since the language that is required to specify the condition in which the disposition is realized is fully as mentalistic as the language that is required to specify the sensations that give rise to the disposition.

Linguistic Arguments for Behaviorism

Thus far, I have discussed a number of arguments that have purported to demonstrate that the truth of behaviorism is somehow a precondition either for the justifiability of knowledge claims about mental states or for the analyticity of certain necessary truths involving mental terms. The arguments to be reviewed next allegedly show that the truth of behaviorism is a precondition for the possibility of learning any language that contains mental terms.

Variants of the following argument are found throughout the literature: In order for it to be possible to teach the use of a word, the tutor must be able to observe whatever regularities are relevant to determining how his student uses the word, for only then can he correct the student's misusages. For example, it is possible to correct a student in his use of such words as "tree" precisely because it is possible to observe whether the things he regularly calls trees are in fact trees. And so on, for other words that designate "publicly observables."

But now consider mental predicates in their first-person employments. In particular, consider the question of how the tutor is to ascertain that the student has grasped the meaning of such locutions as "I have an itch." What the tutor can scrutinize is, if only by definition, the behavior of the student. Hence, unless the tutor is assured of some connection between the correctness of the student's mental ascriptions and the truth of the relevant descriptions of the student's behavior, it will be impossible for him to distinguish those occasions on which the student uses the phrase correctly from those on which he does not. How, in short, is the tutor to tell that his student has mastered the use of "itch" if it is not by noticing the latter's tendency to scratch what he claims to be his itches? And if this is the way it is done, is that not tantamount to saying that the possibility of teaching mental terms depends on the existence of behavioral criteria for the employment of such terms?

It seems clear, however, that the argument does not in fact prove what it started out to prove. For what it succeeds in showing is that the existence of a connection between behavioral and mental ascriptions is a necessary condition for *knowing* that a word has been taught successfully, not for teaching it. And one would suppose it must be at least logically possible to have succeeded in teaching a word even though one acquires no "feedback" whatever from the student; that is, one would suppose that it is logically possible to have succeeded in communicating relevant information to a student about whose correctness of usage one thereafter receives no information. If it is replied that it makes no sense to hold that a student has grasped the meaning of a word, even though nothing about his behavior would indicate that he has done so, then the question is simply begged. For the question that the argument sought to settle was precisely whether, in point of logic, the truth of a mental ascription must be signified by some behavioral trace.[8]

It should be noted further that the condition that the argument seeks to impose would be satisfied if the required connection between mental and behavioral terms were purely contingent. That is, all that is needed in order for us to be certain that a mental word is used correctly is for the occurrence of the state it denotes to be reliably connected to some behavior that is interpersonally observable. It is, of course, true that if the connection is contingent, then we can at best arrive at *moral* certainty that the word has been mastered. Once again, however, it is left to the behaviorist to demonstrate that moral certainty is not, in fact, the best we ever have.

Indeed, the present argument does no more than reduce all arguments over the logical independence of descriptions of behavior from mental ascriptions to arguments over the predicate "has grasped the meaning of a word." Hence, all the arguments that were earlier rehearsed in the discussion of the epistemological character of behaviorism reapply. There are, however, certain special characteristics of assertions that the meaning of a word has been grasped that make it particularly implausible to argue that they could be logically implicated simply by descriptions of the student's verbal behavior.

Suppose we say that in learning the meaning of a word one learns a rule which governs the use of the word. We must then say that in ascertaining whether or not someone has learned the meaning of a word, what one is ascertaining is whether or not he has learned the right rule. That the right rule has been learned is normally established through observation of the student's behavior. Hence, the question whether the behavior of the learner can logically implicate that he has grasped the meaning of a word is equivalent to the question whether any number of observations of his behavior can logically implicate that he is following a certain rule. But clearly no such implication is possible, since the point about a rule is precisely that it determines (would determine) behavior in *indefinitely many* cases, while observation can only ascertain what behavior the student in fact produced on *some definite* (*and perhaps small*) *number* of occasions. In short, ascriptions of rules to speakers, being no more than special cases of inductive inference, share whatever logical fallibility inductive inferences are prone to. I take it to be simply analytic that there can be no sense of "logically implicate" in which the truth of an inductive inference is logically implicated by the data that support it.

Methodological Arguments for Behaviorism

We turn now to a class of arguments in favor of behaviorism that are more directly related to issues in the philosophy of science than those we have so far considered.

It is universally acknowledged that a reasonable condition upon the acceptability of a scientific theory is that it be the simplest among those that are formally capable of accounting for the data. It must also be acknowledged that we do not at present possess a satisfactory, uniform measure of simplicity: that is, one that comes close to consistently giving intuitively plausible results in all the clear cases. The current situation is rather that the simplicity of a theory might reasonably be measured along any of a number of different dimensions, and it is by no means evident that all these measures produce the same ordering. One might, for example, maintain that the simplest theory is the one that recognizes the smallest number of "ultimate" laws (i.e., laws not deducible from covering laws of greater generality), or that the simplest theory is the one that can be specified with the smallest number of terms that denote unobservables, or with the smallest number of symbols in some designated vocabulary, and so on. Nor is it precluded that the most satisfactory definition of simplicity would require some weighted function of a number of such criteria.

Just as it seems plausible to argue that considerations of simplicity require us *ceteris paribus* to prefer a theory that postulates few unobservables to a theory that postulates many, so it may also be maintained that simplicity requires us to prefer a theory in which the terms that designate unobservables are logically connected to observation terms, as against a theory in which they are not. For it seems evident that theories of the latter sort are in some sense potentially more powerful than theories of the former sort, and clearly we must prefer the weaker of two theories when both are capable of accounting for the data.

We can imagine an array of increasingly powerful psychological theories, ordered in terms of increasing liberalization of the connections they permit between theoretical terms and observation terms. The least powerful such theory, and hence the one we would be committed most to prefer, all other things being equal, would presumably be the one in which all theoretical terms are eliminable in favor of observation terms —that is, a strict reductionism. The most powerful such theory, and hence the one we would be committed to prefer least, all other things being equal, would be one in which no theoretical terms are logically connected to any observation terms—that is, a strict realism in which all statements in the theory are independent, except as they are related by rules of formal logic (and, perhaps, by dictionary analyticities of the "Bachelors are unmarried" variety). Intermediate possibilities include theories in which theoretical terms are required to be mapped one-one (or one-many) to observables by correlating semantic rules—for example, theories that, though nonreductive, nevertheless require "criteria" for each of the theoretical terms.

We have been interpreting simplicity principles as rules that tell us which of a pair of competing theories it would be rational to choose, where two theories count as competitive only if they are formally incompatible and both capable of accounting for the known data. But it is also possible to adopt such principles as specifying a priori constraints on the notion of a putative explanation—for example, to decide that one will not regard as acceptable any theory that relaxes beyond a certain point the logical connection between theoretical and behavioral terms. To adopt such a principle in this way is tantamount to adopting what may prove a very strong assumption about the phenomena under investigation: that they are in fact no more complex than may be explained by theories constructed in accordance with the methodological rule in question. For example, to adopt the principle that one will not accept as a putative explanation of behavior any theory in which the theoretical terms are not definable in the observation language is tantamount to assuming that any intervening variable that is employed in the explanation of behavior is in principle eliminable—that is, that one will not in fact encounter behavior of such complexity that the simplest way of explaining it would require the uneliminable employment of an intervening variable.

Now, the important thing about such an assumption is that it is sometimes possible to provide rather convincing evidence of its falsehood. For it is sometimes possible to demonstrate the existence of phenomena the simplest available explanation of which requires the employment of theoretical entities in a way that violates the methodological rule at issue. Thus, in a famous psychological controversy, mediational learning theorists have argued that the phenomena of learning cannot be explained unless we abandon strictly reductive methodological principles in favor of principles that would permit some theoretical entities not eliminable in terms of observables.

It is worth considering one example of the sort of psychological finding that may prove relevant to settling this sort of methodological question. It is well known that, under certain circumstances, conditioning (classical and operant) exhibits limited transitivity. Suppose, for example, that we condition a response B to a stimulus A and a response C to the event B. (Thus, A, B, and C might be paired-associate nonsense syllables, conditioned A-B, B-C.) Under such circumstances, it is relatively easy to demonstrate that presentations of A are significantly likely to produce C as a response, even though the pair A-C has not ever occurred during learning trials.

In such cases, one is very strongly tempted to assume the covert occurrence of B as an "unobserved," "mediating," or "intervening" response. That is, it is natural and plausible to suppose that the subject, upon being provided with A as stimulus, actually produces B as an unobserved response, and that it is this occurrence of B that serves in turn as the stimulus for the observed response C. This view would seem still more plausible if, for example, we could find data indicating that the latency for an overt response C to stimulus B is characteristically shorter than the latency for an overt response C to the stimulus A, for such data would suggest the presence of some intervening operation in the A-C situation that is absent in the B-C situation.

Since we can imagine data that would be directly relevant to the truth of the proposed explanation, it looks as though it is an empirical rather than a methodological question whether the explanation is correct. Yet, the explanation proposed is of a kind to which we are not entitled if we have adopted strict reductionism as a methodological principle. For such a principle requires that we introduce into psychological explanations no theoretical vocabulary that cannot be replaced by terms for observables. Thus there appears to be an impasse: either we give up this explanation (and all other explanations that are logically similar to it), or else we give up the methodological principle.

What we do in fact will, of course, be determined by a number of considerations: how sure we are of the relevant data; how much simplification the employment of explanations of this sort introduces into our general account of behavior (where "simplification" means "simplification as measured by indices other than the degree of logical connectedness between theoretical and observation terms"); what we take to be the precedents in other areas of science, and so on. The important point is that one can easily imagine situations in which it would be rational to abandon the methodological principle rather than the explanation—circumstances in which we would say that the arguments in favor of postulating the mediating response were overwhelming. It is in this rather devious way that our methodological commitments may themselves be required to face the data.

This point is extremely important for a discussion of the methodological arguments concerning behaviorism. It means that we may regard a commitment to behaviorism as involving a speculation about the complexity of those phenomena that psychological explanations will have to account for. This suggests in turn that it may be possible to conceive of circumstances in which the gross facts about the data, together with considerations of naturalness, general economy, and so on might require us to abandon the commitment to behaviorism. For example, if it is possible to demonstrate the occurrence of psychological phenomena for which the simplest available explanation requires us to hypothesize the occurrence of mental events that do not exhibit behavioral correlates, then, since even the weakest variety of behaviorism requires at least that such correlates exist for each type of mental event, we shall be in a situation of forced choice. In particular, we shall be required either to abandon the explanation or else to abandon the methodological principle that forbids explanations of that type.

It is, in fact, easy to find such cases in the psychological literature. The recent display of disenchantment with behaviorism on the part of a number of experimental psychologists is presumably the result of a growing awareness of the methodological significance of these cases.

We shall examine one such case in detail. It has to do with some recent experimentation involving the perception of speech. (The results that are informally discussed below are presented at length by Fodor and Bever [1965] and by Garrett, Bever, and Fodor [1966] where, however, a slightly different experimental paradigm is employed. Readers interested in the details should consult those two papers.)

It is a commonplace to describe speech in a language that one does not know as "torrential." Foreign languages are "spoken in a rush"; foreigners "talk too fast." If, however, one reflects upon the way speech in one's own language sounds, one notes that it appears to come in chunks, separated by pauses of greater or lesser duration. While foreign languages strike the ear as an almost continuous flow of sound, one's own language appears to be segmented in some quite definite way. Moreover, speakers exhibit considerable inter-judge reliability when they are asked to describe the segmentation of particular sentences in their language. For example, they tend to agree on where the longest pauses in a sentence are, or which of two pauses in a sentence is the longer.

This situation is somewhat puzzling. If, as one might suppose, the perception of a pause in speech is simply the perception of a drop in the acoustical energy of the physical speech signal, it is hard to understand why the pausal characteristics of the languages one happens to know should appear to differ from those of languages one does not know. If, on the other hand, the perception of pause is in some way independent of the physical characteristics of the speech signal, it is difficult to understand why speakers agree when they are asked to indicate where the pauses are.

Since pause recognition appears to be in some way contingent upon linguistic competence, and since any clue to the nature of linguistic competence is ipso facto valuable, inquiries have been undertaken into the nature of the perception of pausal segmentation in speech. As a result of these inquiries, it is now possible to give a reasonably convincing account of this aspect of speech perception. That is, we can construct a theory that allows us to predict where the pauses are likely to be heard in speech and what relative length they are likely to be perceived as having. Moreover, this theory enables us to explain both why the perception of pausal structure should be contingent upon linguistic competence and why it should also exhibit the observed interjudge reliability.

The methodologically important point about the theory is this: to accept it is to abandon even the weakest variety of behaviorism since it requires postulating that very abstract and complex mental operations underlie the perception of pausation in speech. Although these operations are, of course, inferred from their behavioral effects (e.g., from the data about where pauses are perceived), there is no serious possibility of assigning individual behaviors as criteria, or even as correlates, to each such operation. Rather, on the view that is incorporated in this theory, the perceived sentence is understood as the product of some very complex integration of the speech signal with linguistic rules. Here, as elsewhere, we cannot associate each operation in the production of a complex artifact with some observable property of the finished product, if only because the traces of earlier operations are sometimes obliterated by the consequences of the later ones. To accept the theory we are about to present is therefore to abandon any methodological principles that require behavioral counterparts for mental events. Conversely, to adhere to methodological behaviorism is to reject this theory, along with whatever explanatory and predictive advantages it affords, and to do so without present hope of replacement.

It appears that the perception of pausation in speech is accounted for by the following generalization: the probability that a pause will be heard at a given point in a sentence is in large part a function of the constituent structure (i.e., of the "parsing") of the sentence at that point and is to that degree independent of the level of acoustic energy of the speech signal. For example, perceptual pauses are more likely to be heard at the syntactic boundaries between words than at those points at which acoustic pauses occur within words. Almost everyone who speaks English will locate a pause in the juncture of the phrase "Bob#Lees," though one can certify by

spectrographic analysis (or, for many speakers, just by care-
fully attending to repetitions of the phrase) that the acoustic
pattern is closer to "Bo#bLees"—that is, that the point of
greatest acoustic energy drop is before the second "b," although the perceptual pause comes before the "L." In cases
like this (and such cases are the norm), the *perceptual,* but
not the *physical,* pause falls at the syntactic juncture. The
syntactic structure is largely independent of the acoustic structure and it is by the former and not by the latter that the percept is determined.

Words are, of course, not the only sorts of syntactic constituents. It can be shown on purely linguistic grounds that
the syntactic analysis of a sentence must involve a parsing
(bracketing) of the sentence into nested units of various
length. Thus, a simple sentence, such as "The man hit the
colorful ball," has roughly the following constituent structure:

((The) (man)) ((hit) ((the) ((colorful) (ball))))

The generalization stated above (that pauses tend to be heard
at constituent boundaries) may be sharpened to predict that
the probability that a pause will be heard at a given point
in a sentence varies with the number of constituents coter-
minous at that point. This turns out to be correct, at least
for the major junctures. Thus, most speakers tend to locate
the longest pause on one or the other side of "hit" in "The
man hit the colorful ball"—although, in acoustic fact, normal
utterances of this sentence contain no major energy drop at
all.

It is at this point that the methodological problems arise.
We have seen that the perception of a pause in a sentence is
not typically a discriminative response to fluctuations in the
acoustic energy of a speech signal. On the contrary, one ap-

parently locates pauses largely by reference to the constituent structure of the sentences in which they are heard. When one perceives a pause in a sentence, what one is perceiving is determined by one's knowledge of the sentence's derived constituent structure.

Assuming then that recognition of the constituent structure is essential to the perception of segmental pause, and assuming too that the analysis of constituent structure is independent of the acoustics, the problem presents itself: How is the constituent structure of a sentence recognized by the persons who hear it?

The general outlines of the answer to this question are now fairly clear. The constituent structure of a sentence is automatically specified by the rules of certain sorts of grammars. Such grammars also have a number of other properties that are clearly related to the capacities actually exhibited by speakers of natural languages: they afford a recursive characterization of the set of grammatical sequences of morphemes, they provide analyses of certain types of structural ambiguity that are exhibited by some sentences of all natural languages, they predict the obligatory stress patterns exhibited in spoken sentences, and so on.

The inference would appear to be that the data processing that is involved in the perception (or, for that matter, in the production) of a sentence in one's own language involves the application of the sort of rules that such grammars formulate. In particular, understanding a sentence in one's native language involves using such rules to assign the appropriate constituent analysis and it is that assignment, in turn, that dictates the perceived pausal segmentation the sentence bears. This hypothesis accounts for the fact that different speakers agree on the location of pauses in the sentences of their language, as well as for the fact that the ability to apprehend such pauses is confined to sentences uttered in a language one understands. For in the former case all speakers of a language presumably employ the same constituent structure rules and in the latter case learning the constituent structure rules for a language is part of learning the language.

But now, what of the operations that are involved in applying such rules? (Or, for that matter, in learning them; the following remarks apply, *mutatis mutandis,* to either performance.) In the first place, it is clear that they are *unconscious* operations, in the sense that they cannot be reported by subjects. Hence the justification for assuming that they occur is largely that they are required by such patterns of explanation as the one just rehearsed. More to the point, it is clear that there are no behavioral *correlates* for such operations and *a fortiori* no behavioral *criteria* for them. That is, just as it is patently false to assume that each assignment of brackets to some stretch of a sentence is associated with some disposition to provide a verbal report of that assignment, so it is also false to assume that such bracketings are associated with characteristic forms of nonverbal behavior. Behavior is produced when the sentence is understood, if it is produced at all; thus, individual mental operations are related to behavior only via the entire computational process of which they form a part. The justification for positing such operations in a psychological explanation can be, then, neither that subjects report their occurrence nor that some nonverbal behavioral index of their occurrence has been observed. Rather, we posit such operations simply because they are required for the construction of an adequate theory of speech perception.

To summarize: what happens when one hears a sentence in a language one knows is apparently that the acoustic signal is integrated by reference to some set of rules that the hearer has internalized during the course of learning the language. This integration is apparently the result of data-handling operations whose output is (*inter alia*) an analysis of the sentence into constituents. How many such operations must take place in the case of a particular sentence, and precisely what transformations are performed upon the acoustic input during the course of such analyses, are problems for psychological and linguistic theory. What is evident, however, is that these operations implicate behavior only in the very indirect sense that they are involved in understanding a sentence; and that, having understood a sentence, the hearer may (or may not) choose to act upon what he has understood.

It should be stressed that the example we have discussed, although perhaps relatively dramatic, is by no means atypical. The literature on the psychology of perception is filled with reports of phenomena whose most persuasive explanation would be precluded by adherence to any substantive form of behaviorism—that is, to any methodological canon about the relation of theoretical to observation terms that amounted to more than a warning against proliferating mental entities beyond necessity. Characteristically, such phenomena have to do with "constancies,"—that is, cases in which normal perception involves radical and uniform departure from the informational content of the physical input. It has been recognized since Helmholtz that such cases provide the best argument for unconscious mental operations, for there appears to be no alternative to invoking such operations if we are to explain the disparity between input and percept.

As we saw in the Introduction, behavioristic accounts of perception as involving the disposition to produce discriminative responses to physical differences among stimuli are plausible only when an isomorphism obtains between perceptual distinctions and specifiable stimulus differences. Where this isomorphism breaks down (as in the failure of perceptual pauses in sentences to correspond to anything that is acoustically marked) some unconscious data processing must be hypothesized. Philosophers who object to such explanations as a matter of principle, as well as philosophers who propose to defend behaviorism on simplicity grounds, would appear to owe a detailed account of these phenomena that avoided mentalistic postulations. The dignified silence that they have so far maintained on such matters does not really amount to an argument.

The Necessity of Mental Events

The previous discussion is intended to suggest that some patterns of explanation in psychology require the hypothesizing of psychological events and processes that may be arbitrarily remote from behavior. This contention, if correct, would appear to be incompatible with adopting any form of behavioristic strictures upon the relation between observation language and theoretical terms in psychological theories.

It is possible to argue, however, that while *psychological mechanisms* may be connected to behavior as remotely as one wishes, it does not follow that mental activities have similar privileges. In particular, it may be argued that there is no reason for thinking of the events that are postulated in psychological explanations of the sort we have been considering as mental events.

This question is, of course, partly terminological. On the one hand, the inferential processes that we have supposed to underlie speech perception must be regarded as unconscious in the strict and unproblematical sense that they cannot be reported by the subject. Now it is possible to maintain that to entertain the notion of an unconscious mental process is either to indulge an incoherence or to implicitly suggest that we redefine "mental." Barring a theory of meaning and of meaning change that would offer some positive support for such claims, it is extremely difficult to know how to tell whether they are in fact true. (Suppose someone were to say that in speaking of "elementary" particles physicists had either contradicted themselves or else had changed the meaning of "particle." How could we tell whether or not he was right?)

On the other hand, two points may be argued in favor of the analogy between the theoretical events of psychological explanation and the mental events of ordinary discourse. The first is that it seems clear that *only* consciousness is at issue. Unlike such unconscious processes as capillary contraction, the kinds of events that are necessary for the comprehension of language are clearly such that if they *were* conscious, one would not hesitate to call them intelligent performances; they would indeed be paradigms of the sort of processes that we describe as "mental." The second point is that the alleged processes eventuate in unequivocally intelligent behavior. The fact that understanding a language is an intellectual achievement provides at least some reason for regarding as mental processes the data processes that it requires.

What, in any event, is *not* an argument against the analogy between psychological and mental events is the claim that the former are "really" neurological transactions. The pattern of explanation discussed above provided evidence for the existence of complex data processes involved in speech perception, but provided no evidence whatever for (or against) analogous neurological processes. It is, of course, possible to claim on independent grounds that the alleged data processes are *in fact* neurological processes. But then, it is equally possible to make that sort of claim about *any* mental events, conscious or otherwise.

One cannot win the argument with a behaviorist, for the position he is defending is that there is "some" sense of "logical connection" in which logical connections between mental terms and behavioral terms must obtain. But how precisely one is to motivate the decision that a given predicate is to count as behavioral is generally left unclear, and the notions of "grammar," "criterion," "definition," and so forth, in terms of which the relation of logical connection is to be explained, remain themselves unexplicated—apparently, as a matter of principle. Indeed, merely to remark that such key concepts must be clarified if any substance is to attach to the claim that they play an essential role in the analysis of psychological explanations is to invite the charge of being pitiably insensitive to the bottomless depths and magical complexity of ordinary language—as though the complexity of the phenomena to be explained could somehow excuse imprecision in the theoretical vocabulary in which the explanation is couched.

Faced with so vaporous a thesis, counterargument can do no better than establish a reasonable prima facie case for mentalism. I have tried to show that nothing goes seriously wrong with the ordinary language of psychological explanation, or with the justification of psychological assertions, if all relevant connections between mental and behavioral terms are assumed to be contingent. Moreover, precisely that assumption is likely to be required for the (perhaps somewhat special) purposes of scientific psychological explanation and, *ceteris paribus,* it would be pleasant if the analysis of ordinary-language mental terms turned out to be reasonably analogous to the analysis of their counterparts in psychology. Finally, it seems evident that behaviorism, considered as an account of theories in psychology, is simply a special case of operationalism considered as an account of scientific theories in general and that the former doctrine ought therefore to share in the discredit that has recently attached to the latter. Insight into the nature of explanation increasingly suggests that the possibility of explanation is independent of the existence of logical connections between theoretical and observational terms. It is enough that we should have *grounds* for applying theoretical terms; we do not also require *criteria*. If this is correct, then the ultimate argument against behaviorism is simply that it seeks to prohibit a priori the employment of psychological explanations that may, in fact, be true.

✺ THREE
Materialism

It is frequently suggested in philosophical discussions of the mind-body problem that it might be reasonable to regard mind states and brain states as contingently identical. How plausible one considers this suggestion to be depends on one's view of an extremely complicated tangle of philosophical problems to which the materialist doctrine is closely connected. Among these are problems that must clearly be faced during the course of providing an account of explanation in psychology.

For example, determining whether or not materialism can be true is part of understanding the relation between theories in psychology and theories in neurology—a relation that many philosophers believe poses a stumbling block for the doctrine of the unity of science. In particular, it is sometimes maintained that the unity of science requires that it prove possible to "reduce" psychological theories to neurological theories, the model of reduction being provided by the relation between constructs in chemistry and those in physics. This is usually taken to mean that, for each theoretical term that appears in psychology, there must be a true statement that articulates a psychophysical identity and that such statements are to be understood on the analogy of statements that identify hydrogen atoms with certain configurations of subatomic particles. On this view, neurological entities are the denotata of psychological terms, just as physical entities are the denotata of chemical terms.[1]

This sort of issue suggests that rather more is at stake when the question of materialism is raised than may initially meet the eye. In this chapter, I shall therefore attempt to bring out some of the logical links between the controversy about materialism and some other problems in philosophical psychology, as well as to survey a number of arguments in which the truth of materialism is directly involved.

Conceptual Background of Contemporary Materialism

Classical empiricism sought to provide a psychological account of the ontogenesis of ideas from which it would follow that the mind could entertain no concept that was not in some sense exemplified in experience. This demonstration has seemed unsatisfactory to contemporary empiricists, who have sought to provide something stronger than psychological necessity for the existence of an experiential component in all coherent concepts.

At its crudest, contemporary empiricism has sought to guarantee an experiential basis of concepts by identifying concept attainment with learning a disposition to provide appropriate verbal and nonverbal responses to specified stimuli. Thus, learning to talk a language is said to involve forming such habits as that of saying "red" when there are red patches, or "pain" upon encountering criterial pain behaviors; paradigmatic of learning to understand a language is learning to bring the slab when someone says "slab."

In its more sophisticated manifestations, contemporary empiricism has argued that a concept is specified, in part, by reference to the kinds of evidence that are typically employed in justifying claims that something falls under that concept. Thus, the connection between the concept *pain* and pain behavior is mediated by a theory according to which giving the meaning of "pain" is, in part, specifying those behaviors that would warrant its application.

Although such versions of empiricism undoubtedly escape the charge of psychologizing, it is less clear that they avoid other traditional objections that have been raised against empiricism in its classic form. In particular, it may plausibly be objected that they fail to provide convincing analyses either of theoretical concepts or of the justification of existential claims about theoretical entities.

Very often, in the natural sciences, an investigator is confronted with a syndrome of observable phenomena, the occurrence of any large proper subset of which provides a reliable basis for the prediction of the remainder, even though it is implausible to argue that any of the phenomena cause any of the others. In such cases, the relevant form of explanation often consists in postulating some unobserved processes, events, or states to whose agency the occurrence of the syndrome is directly or indirectly attributable.

A number of factors may be relevant to determining whether such a postulation is warranted. Among these are the extent to which the data permit the elaboration of an account of theoretically interesting relations among the unobservables (as, e.g., dominance or connectedness in genetic theory, or valence in chemistry); the extent to which the postulations license inferences about those observables that are not included in the initial syndrome (as, e.g., the prediction of the phenomena of perceptual defense on the basis of the Freudian postulation of a censorship mechanism), and so on.

Materialism and Inferred Entities

The relevance of these remarks is that it is sometimes suggested that certain uses of psychological language in ordinary and technical discourse may be understood on the model of theoretical postulations in science. On the suggested analogy, behavior takes on the role of the observed syndrome and some mental event or state corresponds to the inferred entity.[2] According to this account then, learning to use everyday psychological language involves being introduced to the culturally accepted views concerning *which* mental states are involved in the etiology of which behaviors. Applying psychological predicates in the second person is then a case of making the inferences that are licensed by those views. The use of mental terms in scientific theories is thus held to be continuous with certain of their ordinary language uses, except that, in psychology, mental terms are explicitly taken to designate theoretical entities, and the explanations in which such terms figure are explicitly subject to conditions of simplicity and rigor.

Advocates of this position argue that it makes sense of the relations between, for example, talk about pain behavior and talk about pain in a way in which neither behaviorism nor dualism manages to. On the one hand, the inferred-entity account, when held in conjunction with a realistic interpretation of theoretical terms, makes it clear why behaviorists have failed to demonstrate the logical sufficiency of statements about behavior for psychological statements: existential statements about theoretical entities are *always* logically independent of statements about the observable data. On the other hand, the present suggestion accounts for the peculiar intimacy of the relation between statements about behavior and statements about mental states, in a way in which dualistic theories do not. For if ϕs are, in the first instance, entities that are postulated in order to explain the ϕ-behavior syndrome, it is evident that the occurrence of the ϕ-behavior syndrome must provide the best possible prima facie evidence for ascriptions of ϕ.

The suggestion that the justification of second-person mental ascriptions is analogous to the justification of existential claims about theoretical entities must be sharply distinguished from the traditional claim that second-person mental ascriptions are somehow based upon analogies. The latter view is, perhaps, best interpreted as an ontogenetic hypothesis about how we might in fact come to entertain the suspicion that the behavior of other people is contingent upon antecedent or concurrent mental states, processes, and events: having noted that our own behavior has such antecedents, and having taken note of the similarity between the behavior we produce and the behavior of other people, we hypothesize correspondingly similar mental operations.

It is unclear that this speculation is either logically coherent or psychologically plausible. But even if it is a fact that no one who had never himself had pains or intentions would think of ascribing them to others, that fact would be largely irrelevant to the *justification* of such ascriptions. Traditional objections to the "argument" from analogy have correctly maintained that it is a poor inductive extrapolation that must base itself upon one case. This consideration does not, however, impugn the inferred-entity account of second-person psychological ascriptions. For if we distinguish between discovery and justification, we may correspondingly distinguish between the occasion that suggests the attribution of pains to others (conceivably having a pain oneself) and the character of the justification for such attributions (viz., that they provide the simplest systematic account of what one observes about other people's behavior).

I do not wish here to discuss the question of whether or not mental entities are plausibly treated as inferred entities. But it is important to understand the consequences of assuming that they are, since these consequences bear upon the truth of materialism in a way that has not previously been noted. I shall argue that it is not an historical accident but a simple consideration of coherence that accounts for the fact that the inferred-entity view of how one justifies the application of mental predicates is invariably held in conjunction with a materialist view of their denotata.

Ontological Status of Inferred Entities

A reasonable reaction to the suggestion that mental states are profitably compared to theoretical entities is to remark upon its prima facie unnaturalness. Among the paradigms of theoretical entities are, for example, the microparticles of physics. But what, after all, do pains and photons have in common?

However, this line of thought badly misses the point. For to say that the referent of a term is a theoretical entity is not to provide an ontological classification—that is, is not to say what *kind* of entity it is. Rather, it is to emphasize the way in which existence claims about that entity are justified. If there are trees on Mars, then such trees are theoretical entities. Not because the putative Martian flora are in some way more mysterious or less substantial than our own, but only because our information about them is (currently) arrived at by inferences from spectroscopic analyses, seasonal color changes, and so on. At the moment when observational investigation of the Martian landscape does become possible, then existential claims about Martian trees will ipso facto become verifiable by observation, and Martian trees will ipso facto cease to be theoretical entities.[3]

Since whether or not we say of an entity that it is inferred is a question solely of the sort of justificatory arguments we use to substantiate claims about its existence, the line between observed and inferred entities is just as hard to draw as the line between observation and inference. It is, indeed, the same line. I think that there is a strong temptation to say that the larger viruses are not inferred entities *any more*— specifically because of the electron microscope. Yet it is possible to maintain that the argument from shadows on the plate to viruses on the slide is fully as complex as the argument from spectroscopic results to vegetation on Mars. What we decide to call an observation is in part determined by what we feel comfortable about calling an instrument of observation. Places in which telescopes are employed are called observatories for reasons that are not unrelated to the fact that no one would want to hold the craters on the moon to be theoretical entities.

I have said that the line between observation and inference is hard to *draw*, not that it is hard to stipulate. One can always decide that certain predicates, and only those, constitute one's "observation vocabulary." The difficulty lies, notoriously, in justifying such decisions. If the present view of the distinction between theoretical and observed entities is deflationary, that is because the previous attempts to draw the line between observation and inference at some epistemologically interesting point—for example, by holding that only terms for "qualia" are to count as observation terms—have uniformly proved too weak to provide an acceptable account of the justification of claims about theoretical entities, even in well-entrenched scientific theories.[4]

It appears that there is no a priori answer to the question "Where does a theory confront the data?" In principle, any nonlogical term in the vocabulary of a theory is a possible observation term. So long as no law of nature prohibits the observation of what a term denotes, whether or not observations of its denotata do in fact play a role in the confirmation of some theory depends solely upon our ingenuity in inventing instruments of observation and in devising experiments in which such instruments may be deployed. So far no philosopher has provided very convincing reasons for dismissing as a *façon de parler* scientists' occasional claims to have observed chromosomes, microparticles, distant nebulae, and so on, or for supposing that there is need for a strict sense of "strictly," in terms of which what was strictly observed in such cases were only patches and traces.

Realism and Materialism

If, as we have supposed, the claim that *T* is an inferred entity is a de facto claim about the way in which existential statements about *T*s are in fact justified, certain conclusions follow that are directly relevant to the inferred-entity view of psychological terms. In particular, if the assertion that *T* is an inferred entity is logically equivalent to the assertion that the sorts of arguments that are used to establish its existence do not in fact include reference to alleged observations of *T*s, then the claim that *T* is an inferred entity can be true *only where it is logically possible to observe* (makes sense to speak of observing) *that something is a T*. Another way of making the same point is that on a realistic analysis of theoretical entities it makes no sense to say that something is *necessarily* a theoretical entity, since statements of the form "*T* has not been observed" are never analytic in cases in which *T* ranges over physical entities, states, events, and so on.

On this analysis, claims about *inferences* to T can be true only where talk about *observations* of T makes sense. It is this consequence of the realistic view of theoretical entities that has serious implications for the inferred-entity account of second-person psychological ascriptions. For, so far, the inferred-entity account has not provided for the possibility, in principle, of the observational verification of such ascriptions. On the contrary, it looks as though the claim is that the existence of other people's psychological states is *necessarily* inferred since, prima facie, there is no sense in talking of directly observing other people's mental states. If, however, "X observationally verified the truth of P" is logically false wherever P is a second-person psychological ascription, then it follows that the claim that psychological entities are inferred entities is simply the denial of a necessarily false statement and hence itself necessarily true. But this in turn entails that the notion of a theoretical term is somehow being misused when second-person psychological predicates are likened to such terms since, as we have just seen, it is characteristic of bona fide theoretical entities that statements asserting that they *are* theoretical entities must invariably be contingent.

It should be emphasized that the present argument is not impugned by the fact that there is a perfectly good ordinary-language use of such remarks as "X observed that Y was in pain." For the whole point about the inferred-entity view is that it offers an analysis of such remarks according to which they too announce inferential judgments. That is, according to the inferred-entity view, the cases in which we (properly, but colloquially) claim to have directly observed that some psychological predicate applies are simply those cases in which our (presumably unconscious) inferences from behavior to psychological state are based on unusually good evidence—for example, in which a very substantial or very reliable part of the behavior syndrome that is characteristically associated with the psychological state is on view. Now the present argument claims that for there to be any sense to the assertion that the justification of a certain existential statement in a theory is inferential there must be something that that theory would, in principle, count as a corresponding observational justification of that statement. But the inferred-entity theory does not count as observations those verifications of second-person mental ascriptions that would be described as observational in ordinary language.

The argument that we have been considering does not by any means show that the inferred-entity account of second-person mental ascriptions is false. But it does show that that account is incoherent unless some sense can be given to the notion of direct observational verification of such ascriptions. And, as far as I can see, saying that the inferred-entity view must assign some sense to the notion of an observational confirmation of second-person psychological ascriptions is tantamount to saying that whoever holds the inferred-entity view is committed to some form of materialism. For if some statements of psychophysical identities are true, it could be claimed that some neurological observations would count as noninferential verifications of second-person mental ascriptions. If X has observed the neurological event N, and N is identical with the mental event E, it follows that X has observed E. (I assume—what is by no means obvious—that there is some sense of "observe" in which it is not intensional.) On the other hand, if one assumes that *no* psychophysical identity statements are true, it is extremely unclear what other candidates for observational verifications of second-person mental ascriptions the inferred-entity view could possibly offer.

Arguments Against Materialism

Problems about materialism are thus linked with other problems currently central in the philosophy of mind. We shall presently see that they also involve some rather general issues in the theory of language. In the remainder of this chapter, we shall examine a number of questions about the status of the psychophysical identity statements in terms of which materialism is articulated. We turn first to a discussion of what is perhaps the most important argument for the view that no statement of the form "*x* is *y*" could be significant where *x* is a mental term, *y* is a physiological term, "is" means identity, and all terms bear their current senses.

This argument bases itself upon an appeal to an extended form of a principle of logic known as Leibniz' Law. Leibniz' Law states that no proposition of the form "*x* is identical with *y*" can be true unless, for each nonintensional predicate F, $Fx \equiv Fy$. That is, the law states that if *x* is identical with *y*, then every nonintensional predicate true of *x* is also true of *y* and vice versa.

Now it has frequently been suggested that Leibniz' Law can be extended to provide a further condition upon the truth of identity statements. In particular what has been called the Law of Transferable Epithets states that if *x* is identical with *y*, and if *Fx* makes sense (is linguistically possible), then *Fy* must also make sense (be linguistically possible).

If the Law of Transferable Epithets is true, it would appear to have some serious implications for materialistic accounts of mental predicates. For example, it clearly makes sense to say that the firing of neuron *N* took place three inches from the base of Smith's skull. Therefore, according to the Law of Transferable Epithets, the firing of neuron *N* could not be identical with, say, one of Smith's wishes unless it also made sense to say that the wish took place three inches from the base of his skull. But since this latter remark is alleged to be nonsensical, it follows that the program of identifying wishes with neural events must be abandoned.

Three kinds of moves can be made against this argument; I am not at this point certain whether any of them is successful.

In the first place, it may simply be denied that such statements as "The wish happened three inches from the base of his skull" are properly described as absurd, nonsensical, and so on. For, it may be said, even though such statements certainly *sound* odd, no violation of a linguistic rule is involved in making them. Analogously, it might be said that the oddity of claiming that one craves a cool refreshing drink of H_2O is not an argument against the chemical theory of water. For, though that would be an odd-sounding thing to claim to crave, the oddity presumably cannot be traced to the violation of any rule of language.

The argument hinges on the fact that it is in general not clear which of the indefinitely many regularities that are true of our use of a word ought to be attributed to the operation of the rules that determine the meaning of the word.[5] Thus, it is perhaps a statistically certifiable regularity about "H_2O" that it is more often used by persons who possess a high-school degree than by persons who do not. But, clearly, no one would suppose that that regularity is in any sense a consequence of a linguistic rule governing the use of "H_2O," or that the fact that that regularity obtains contributes in any sense to the meaning "H_2O." Similarly, it is a regularity about "H_2O" that it is characteristically used in technical contexts. But it is by no means obvious that departing from that regularity ought to be counted as inventing a new sense of "H_2O." Nor is it a good argument against the identification of H_2O with water that references to the latter occur in contexts in which references to the former would be odd.

By parity of argument, according to the materialist, oddities may result when one departs from the regularity that predicates of spatial location are not to be applied to such terms as "wish." But unless it is demonstrated that such departures constitute violations of the meaning rules of English, the oddities they engender provide no case against those psychophysical identity statements in which "wish" appears. Still less do they indicate that allowing the application of spatial predicates to wishes ipso facto constitutes an equivocation on "wish."

This is one of the points, it seems to me, at which the philosopher must find his lack of a general theory of the semantics of natural languages most vexing. In the absence of a well-motivated account of the differences between those regularities that are the consequence of a speaker's adherence to meaning rules and those that are not, it is hard to see what ought to be deduced from the truth of the allegation that a given way of talking is odd. Correspondingly, in the absence of a well-motivated account of change of meaning, it is hard to know how to decide when departing from a regularity that some word obeys amounts to an implicit equivocation on the word. It should be emphasized that appeals to the naïve intuitions of speakers can be of relatively little use in deciding these issues—first, because the cases about which philosophers disagree are, not surprisingly, precisely those cases about which intuition tends to be unclear; second, because we have no way of distinguishing those intuitions that can properly be attributed to the informant's linguistic mastery from those that stem from his philosophical commitments. No doubt we ought to believe an informant who tells us that it sounds odd to attribute places to wishes; but must we also believe him when he intuits that the source of the oddity is linguistic? [6] (Needless to say, this question is also pertinent when one serves as one's own informant.)

In short, the materialist can correctly argue that the fact that a way of talking is odd is not a conclusive reason for abandoning the premises that lead one to talk that way. His antagonist can reply, equally plausibly, that it is at best not clear that the materialist is talking sense when he states a psychophysical identity and that one ought, in general, to avoid ways of talking that may be nonsensical. Barring an account of meaning on which both sides can agree, the argument would appear to rest there.

A more interesting line of defense for the materialist would perhaps be to deny that the putative Law of Transferable Epithets is valid. That is, he might both maintain that there are circumstances in which it would be rational to accept an identification that violated that law and deny that such circumstances invariably involve fallacies of equivocation.

The point to be noted rests on an asymmetry between Leibniz' Law and the Law of Transferable Epithets. In particular, the denial of Leibniz's Law trivially implies contradictions if we permit substitutivity of identity to operate as usual. That is, from Fx and not Fy and "x is identical with y," it is possible to derive both Fx and *not* Fx. Our grounds for refusing to accept any identification that violates Leibniz' Law are thus as good as our grounds for requiring arguments to be consistent.

However, no corresponding consideration holds in the case of the Law of Transferable Epithets. In particular, from the premises that "The form of words 'Fx' makes sense," "x is identical with y," and "The form of words 'Fy' makes no sense," no contradiction follows. Substitutivity of identity does not hold across quotation marks, roughly because what makes sense depends upon what linguistic conventions have in fact been adopted, and it is surely logically possible that conventions should have been adopted for *"Fx,"* and that *x* should in fact be identical with *y*, yet that no conventions should have been adopted for *"Fy."*

One might put it that "We say————" and "We do not say————" are themselves intensional contexts. It is therefore hardly surprising that Leibniz' Law should fail to hold for terms that occur in those contexts.

Given the possibility in principle of violating the Law of Transferable Epithets, it is not too hard to find cases in the history of science where it is tempting to say that that law was in fact violated. It appears that scientific discoveries do sometimes provide for ways of talking to which no sense could previously have been assigned. Nor is it invariably evident in such cases that the intuitively correct analysis is that the meanings of key terms have been altered.

It seems clear, for example, that prior to the adoption of atomic theories of matter, no definite sense could have been attached to the claim that the smallest sample of water is larger than the smallest sample of hydrogen, or to any similar assertion. I suppose it would now be universally admitted, on the one hand, that some such claims are meaningful and true, and, on the other, that it is implausible to say that words like "water" underwent a change of meaning when the atomic theory was adopted. Similarly, it is often noted that it requires the assumption that the Earth is round in order to render coherent speculations about the distance around the Earth. Here again, it is hard to see how a case could be made for an interpretation on which the sentence "The Earth is round" is equivocal. For that would presumably entail that there is or was one sense of "Earth" in which "The Earth is round" is logically false and one sense of

"Earth" in which "The Earth is round" is logically true so that, in either sense, to make the empirical discovery that the Earth is round is logically impossible.

There remains to be discussed one further counter to the use of the Law of Transferable Epithets in order to demonstrate the incoherence of statements that articulate psychophysical identities. It may plausibly be suggested that the materialist's apparent violation of the Law of Transferable Epithets derives not from supposing that there are true psychophysical identity statements, but rather from supposing that the variables in such statements range over *entities*. In particular, on the present view, the materialist thesis should be so formulated as to involve mental and physiological *states*. Thus, a typical psychophysical identity statement would be "Having a wish is being in such and such a physiological condition" rather than "A wish is such and such a physiological condition." Since, for example, spatial predicates do not apply to states but to the entities that are in them ("John is three feet from the door," but not "Having an inflamed tonsil is three feet from the door"), such predicates will apply to *neither* the neurological *nor* the mental terms that are involved in psychophysical identity statements; hence the strictures upon the transferability of epithets will be trivially satisfied by such statements.

If there is a difficulty with this sort of suggestion, it is that it places a restriction upon the grammar of statements that relate neurological and psychological terms that is not satisfied by paradigm cases of statements that clearly do articulate theoretical identifications. Consider, for example, colds. It is true to say that having a cold is just having a certain set of symptoms with a certain etiology. That is, there is a state-to-state identification between colds and physiological conditions that is analogous to the state-to-state identifications that we are supposing may obtain for wishes and neurological conditions. But in the case of colds it is proper to say that *since* having a cold is just being in a certain condition, it follows that a cold is just that condition. That is, we are committed both to "Having a cold is having a certain set of symptoms with a certain etiology," *and* to "A cold is a certain set of symptoms with a certain etiology," *and* to the principle that the former of these statements entails the latter. If, however, we allow the same inference in the case of psychological states and physiological states—for example, if we are allowed to infer that since having a pain is just being in such and such a physiological state, it follows that the pain is just that state—we find ourselves once again committed to locutions that are in apparent violation of the Law of Transferable Epithets.

In short, the suggestion that psychophysical identities be construed as state-to-state identities does manage to provide a way of holding a materialist view without violating the strictures on transferability. But it does so at the price of an apparently arbitrary restriction against employing a form of inference that otherwise appears to be valid: the inference from "Having an X is just being in state Y" to "an X is a Y."

It seems to me that, on balance, the case against the possibility that some psychophysical identity statements are significant has not been proved. Nor does it seem that the dispute is likely to be settled until more insight has been gained into the criteria for meaning change in natural languages on the one hand, and, on the other, into the relation between meaning change and theoretical revision in the empirical sciences. That both problems are likely to be difficult is indicated by the consideration that the first directly involves the distinction between analytic and synthetic propositions, while the second involves questions about the conventional status of scientific theories and laws.

Materialism and the Relation between
Psychology and Neurology

For purposes of the present investigation, we are primarily interested in materialism as it bears upon problems
about psychological explanation. We need, therefore, to
clarify the implications of the materialist view for an account
of the relations between psychological and neurological
theories. I shall argue that while it is by no means evident
that materialism must be regarded as conceptually incoherent,
it is equally unclear that the truth of materialism would entail
the views of the relation between psychology and neurology
that have often been held in conjunction with it. In particular,
to claim that mind states and brain states are contingently
identical need not be to hold that psychological theories are
reducible to neurological theories. Nor would the truth of
materialism entail that the relevant relation between psychological and neurological constructs is that the latter provide
"microanalyses" of the former. It is to these issues that we
now proceed.

Let us commence by trying to form some picture of how
the problem of the relation between psychology and neurology
emerges during the course of attempts to provide systematic
scientific explanations of behavior.

Such attempts have characteristically exhibited two phases
that, although they may be simultaneous in point of history,
are nevertheless distinguishable in point of logic. In the first
phase, the psychologist attempts to arrive at theories that
provide what are often referred to as "functional" characterizations of the mechanisms responsible for the production
of behavior. To say that the psychologist is seeking functional
characterizations of psychological constructs is at least to
say that, in this phase of explanation, the criteria employed
for individuating such constructs are based primarily upon

hypotheses about the role they play in the etiology of behavior. Such hypotheses are constrained by two general considerations. On the one hand, by the principle that the psychological states, processes, and so on hypothesized to be
responsible for the production of behavior must be supposed
to be sufficiently complex to account for whatever behavioral
capacities the organism can be demonstrated to possess; on
the other, by the principle that specific aspects of the character of the organism's behavior must be explicable by
reference to specific features of the hypothesized underlying
states and processes or of their interactions.

Thus, for example, a psychologist might seek to explain
failures of memory by reference to the decay of a hypothetical
memory "trace," an attempt being made to attribute to the
trace properties that will account for such observed features
of memory as selectivity, stereotyping, and so forth. As
more is discovered about memory—for example, about the
effects of pathology upon memory, or about differences between "short-" and "long-term" memory—the properties
attributed to the trace, and to whatever other psychological
systems are supposed to interact with it, must be correspondingly elaborated. It is, of course, the theorist's expectation
that, at some point, speculations about the character of the
trace will lead to confirmable experimental predictions about
previously unnoticed aspects of memory, thus providing independent evidence for the claim that the trace does in fact
have the properties it is alleged to have.

To say that, in the first phase of psychological explanation, the primary concern is with determining the functional
character of the states and processes involved in the etiology
of behavior is thus to say that, at that stage, the hypothesized
psychological constructs are individuated primarily or solely
by reference to their alleged causal consequences. What one
knows (or claims to know) about such constructs is the

effects their activity has upon behavior. It follows that phase-one psychological theories postulate functionally equivalent mechanisms when and only when they postulate constructs of which the behavioral consequences are, in theoretically relevant respects, identical.

This sort of point has sometimes been made by comparing first-phase psychological theories with descriptions of a "machine table"—that is, of the sets of directions for performing computations—of a digital computer. Neurological theories, correspondingly, are likened to descriptions of the "hardware"; that is, of the physical machinery into which such tables are programmed.[7] Since two physical realizations of the same table—that is, two computers capable of performing the mathematically identical set of computations in mathematically identical ways—may differ arbitrarily in their physical structure, mathematical equivalence is independent of physical similarity: two machines may, in this sense, share functionally equivalent "psychological" mechanisms even though they have neither parts nor configurations of parts in common.

The second phase of psychological explanation has to do with the specification of those biochemical systems that do, in fact, exhibit the functional characteristics enumerated by phase-one theories. The image that suggests itself to many psychologists is that of opening a "black box": having arrived at a phase-one theory of the kinds of operations performed by the mechanisms that are causally responsible for behavior, one then "looks inside" to see whether or not the nervous system does in fact contain parts capable of performing the alleged functions. The situation is more complicated, however, than this image suggests since the notion of a "part," when applied to the nervous systems of organisms, is less than clear. The physiological psychologist's task of determining what, if any, organization into subsystems the nervous system of an organism exhibits is precisely the problem of determining whether the nervous system has subsystems whose functional characteristics correspond with those required by antecedently plausible psychological theories.

The two phases of psychological explanation thus condition one another. On the one hand, it is clear that a psychological theory that attributes to an organism a state or process that the organism has no physiological mechanisms capable of realizing is ipso facto incorrect. If memory is a matter of forming traces, then there must be subsystems of the nervous system that are capable of going from one steady state to another and that are capable of remaining in the relevant states for periods that are at least comparable to known retention periods. If no such mechanisms exist, then the trace is the wrong model for the functional organization of memory.

On the other hand, the relevant notion of a neurological subsystem is that of a biochemical mechanism whose operation can correspond to some state or process that is postulated by a satisfactory psychological theory. To say that the goals of physiological psychology are set by the attempt to find mechanisms that correspond to certain functions is to say that it is the psychological theory that articulates these functions that determines the principle of individuation for neurological mechanisms. Once again, analogies to the analysis of less complicated systems may be helpful. What makes a carburetor part of an engine is not the spatial contiguity of its own parts (the parts of fuel injectors exhibit no such contiguity) nor is it the homogeneity of the materials of which it is composed. It is rather the fact that its operation corresponds to a function that is detailed in the theory of internal-combustion engines and that there is no sub- or superpart of the carburetor whose operation corresponds to that function.

The problem, then, is one of fit and mutual adjustment:

on the one hand, there is a presumed psychological theory, which requires possibly quite specific, complex, and detailed operations on the part of the neurological mechanisms that underlie behavior; on the other hand, there is a putative articulation of the nervous system into subsystems that must be matched to these functional characteristics and that must also attempt to maximize anatomical, morphological, and biochemical plausibility. This extremely complex situation is sometimes abbreviated by materialist philosophers into the claim that identification between psychological and neurological states is established on the basis of constant correlation and simplicity. We have seen that it is an open question whether the relevant relation is identification. Our present point is that the evidence required to justify postulating the relation is something considerably more complex than mere correlation. It is rather a nice adjustment of the psychological characterization of function to considerations of neurological plausibility, and vice versa.

Microanalysis and Functional Analysis

This discussion of the way in which psychological and neurological theories integrate during the course of the development of scientific explanations of behavior is, to be sure, no more than the barest sketch. But, insofar as the sketch is at all plausible, it suggests that the reductivist view of the relation between psychological and neurological theories is seriously misleading, even if one accepts a materialistic account of the relation between psychological and neurological constructs. The suggestion is that if materialism is true, a completed account of behavior would contain statements that identify certain neural mechanisms as having functions detailed during the course of phase-one theory construction and that some such statements would hold for each psychological construct. But such statements, clearly, are quite different in kind from those that articulate paradigmatic cases of reductive analysis.

This distinction seems to have been pretty widely missed by materialists, particularly in the literature that relates discussions of materialism to problems about the unity of science. Oppenheim and Putnam, for example, are explicit in referring to neurological theories, such as those of Hebb, as constituting "micro-reductions" of the corresponding psychological theories of memory, learning, motivation, and so on. On the Oppenheim-Putnam account, "the essential feature of micro-reduction is that the branch [of science] B_1 [which provides the micro-reduction of B_2] deals with the parts of the objects dealt with by B_2." [8]

Our present point is that it is difficult to understand how this could be the correct model for the relation between psychological and neurological theories. Psychological entities (sensations, for example) are not readily thought of as capable of being microanalyzed into *anything,* least of all neurons or states of neurons. Pains do not have parts, so brain cells are not parts of pains.

It is, in short, conceivable that there may be true psychophysical identity statements, but it seems inconceivable that such statements are properly analyzed as expressing what Place (1956) has called identities of composition, that is, as expressing relations between wholes and their parts. It should be emphasized that not all statements of identities *are* identities of composition. Compare "Her hat is a bundle of straw" with "He is the boy I knew in Chicago."

It is worth pursuing at some length the difference between the present view of the relation between psychological and neurological constructs and the view typical of reductivist materialism. In reductive analysis (microanalysis), one asks: "What does X consist of?" and the answer has the form of a specification of the microstructure of *X*s. Thus: "What does water consist of?" "Two atoms of hydrogen linked with one atom of oxygen." "What does lightning consist of?" "A stream of electrons." And so on. In typical cases of functional analysis, by contrast, one asks about a part of a mechanism *what role it plays* in the activities that are characteristic of the mechanism as a whole: "What does the camshaft do?" "It opens the valves, permitting the entry into the cylinder of fuel, which will then be detonated to drive the piston." Successful microanalysis is thus often contingent upon the development of powerful instruments of observation or precise methods of dissection. Successful functional analysis, on the other hand, requires an appreciation of the sorts of activity that are characteristic of a mechanism and of the contribution made by the functioning of each part of the mechanism to the economy of the whole.

Since microanalysis and functional analysis are very different ways of establishing relations between scientific theories, or between ordinary-language descriptions, conceptual difficulties may result when the vocabulary of one kind of analysis is confounded with the vocabulary of the other.

If I speak of a device as a "camshaft," I am implicitly identifying it by reference to its physical structure, and so I am committed to the view that it exhibits a characteristic and specifiable decomposition into physical parts. But if I speak of the device as a "valve lifter," I am identifying it by reference to its function and I therefore undertake no such commitment. There is, in particular, no sense to the question "What does a valve lifter consist of?" if this is understood as a request for microanalysis—that is, as analogous to such questions as "What does water consist of?" (There *is*, of course, sense to the question "What does *this* valve lifter consist of?" but the generic valve lifter must be *functionally* defined, and functions do not have parts.) One might put it that being a valve lifter is not reducible to (is not a matter of) being a collection of rods, springs, and atoms, in the sense in which being a camshaft is. The kinds of questions that it makes sense to ask about camshafts need not make sense, and are often impertinent, when asked about valve lifters.

It is, then, conceivable that serious confusions could be avoided if we interpreted statements that relate psychological and neurological constructs not as articulating microanalyses but as attributing certain psychological functions to corresponding neurological systems. For example, philosophers and psychologists who have complained that it is possible to trace an input from afferent to central to efferent neurological systems without once encountering motives, strategies, drives, needs, hopes, along with the rest of the paraphernalia of psychological theories, have been right in one sense but wrong in another, just as one would be if one argued that a complete mechanical account of the operation of an internal-combustion engine never encounters such a thing as a valve lifter. In both cases, the confusion occurs when a term that properly figures in functional accounts of mechanisms is confounded with terms that properly appear in mechanistic accounts, so that one is tempted to think of the function of a part as though it were itself one part among others.

From a functional point of view, a camshaft is a valve lifter and *this* valve lifter (i.e., this particular mechanism for lifting valves) may be "nothing but" a camshaft. But a mechanistic account of the operations of internal-combustion engines does not seek to replace the concept of a valve lifter with the concept of a camshaft, nor does it seek to "reduce" the former to the latter. What it does do is to explain *how* the valves get lifted: that is, what mechanical transactions are involved when the camshaft lifts the valves. In the same way, presumably, neurological theories seek to explain what

biochemical transactions are involved when drives are reduced, motives entertained, objects perceived, and so on.

In short, drives, motives, strategies, and such are, on
the present view, internal states postulated in attempts to
account for behavior, perception, memory, and other phenomena in the domain of psychological theories. In completed accounts, they could presumably serve to characterize
the functional aspects of neurological mechanisms; that is,
they would figure in explanations of how such mechanisms
operate to determine the molar behavior of an organism, its
perceptual capacities, and so on. But this does not entail that
drives, motives, and strategies have microanalyses in terms
of neurological systems any more than valve lifters can be
microanalyzed into camshafts.

There are still further philosophically pertinent differences
between the suggestion that psychophysical identity statements should be understood as articulating functional analyses
and the suggestion that they should be analyzed as micro-
reductions.

When, in paradigmatic cases, entities in one theory are
reduced to entities in another, it is presupposed that both
theories have available conceptual mechanisms for saying
what the entities have in common. For example, given that
water can be "reduced" to H_2O, it is possible to say what
all samples of water have in common either in the language
of viscosity, specific gravity, and so on at the macrolevel, or
in chemical language at the microlevel. It is patent that
functional analysis need not share this property of reductive
analysis. When we identify a certain mousetrap with a certain
mechanism, we do not thereby commit ourselves to the possibility of saying in mechanistic terms what all members
of the set of mousetraps have in common. Because it is
(roughly) a sufficient condition for being a mousetrap that

a mechanism be customarily *used* in a certain way, there is nothing in principle that requires that a pair of mousetraps *have* any shared mechanical properties. It is, indeed, because "mousetrap" is functionally rather than mechanically defined that "building a better mousetrap"—that is, building a mechanically novel mousetrap, which functions better than conventional mousetraps do—is a reasonable goal to set oneself.

It is a consequence of this consideration that the present interpretation of the relation between neurological and psychological constructs is compatible with very strong claims about the ineliminability of mental language from behavioral theories. Let us suppose that there are true psychophysical statements that identify certain neurological mechanisms as the ones that possess certain psychologically relevant functional properties. It still remains quite conceivable that identical psychological functions could sometimes be ascribed to anatomically heterogeneous neural mechanisms. In that case, mental language will be required to state the conditions upon such ascriptions of functional equivalence. It is, in short, quite conceivable that a parsing of the nervous system by reference to anatomical or morphological similarities may often fail to correspond in any uniform way to its parsing in terms of psychological function. Whenever this occurs, explicit reference to the character of such functions will be required if we are to be able to say what we take the brain states that we classify together to have in common.

Every mousetrap can be identified with some mechanism, and being a mousetrap can therefore be identified with being a member of some (indefinite) set of possible mechanisms. But enumerating the set is not a way of dispensing with the notion of a mousetrap; that notion is required to say what all the members of the set have in common and, in particular, what credentials would be required to certify a putative new member as belonging to the set.

Such considerations may be extended to suggest not only that a *plausible* version of materialism will need to view psychological theories as articulating the functional characteristics of neural mechanisms, but also that that is the *only* version of materialism that is likely to prove coherent. Consider the following argument, which Sellars has offered as a refutation of materialism:

Suppose I am experiencing a circular red raw feel . . . (in certain cases) the most careful and sophisticated introspection will fail to refute the following statement: "There is a finite subregion ΔR of the raw feel patch ψr, and a finite time interval Δt, such that during Δt no property of ΔR changes."

The refutation may now proceed by appeal to Leibniz' Law. Suppose there is a brain state ϕ_r which is held to be identical with the psychological state ψ_r that one is in when one senses something red (i.e., with the "red raw feel"). Then substitution of ϕ_r for ψ_r permits the inference: there is a finite region ΔR of the brain state ϕ_r and a finite time interval Δt, such that during Δt no property of ΔR changes.

But this, as even pre-Utopian neurophysiology shows us, is factually false. . . . Thus, during, say, 500 milliseconds, the 5° region at the center of my phenomenal circle does not change in any property, whereas no region of the physical brain-event can be taken small enough such that *none* of its properties change during a 500-millisecond period.[9]

The point of this argument is, I think, entirely independent of its appeal to such dubious psychological entities as "red raw feels." For it seems pretty clear that the principles we employ for individuating neurological states are in general different from, and logically independent of, those that we employ for individuating psychological states. Since what counts as one sensation, one wish, one desire, one drive, and so on is not specified by reference to the organism's neurophysiology, it seems hardly surprising that an organism may persist in a given psychological condition while undergoing neurological change. If a materialist theory is so construed as to deny this, then materialism is certain to prove *contingently* false.

Nor does Sellars' argument depend solely upon the possibility of there being differences in "grain" between neurological and psychological variation. The problem is not just that slight changes in neurophysiology may be compatible with continuity of psychological state. It is rather that we have no right to assume a priori that the nervous system may not sometimes produce indistinguishable psychological effects by *radically* different physiological means. How much redundancy there may be in the nervous system is surely an open empirical question. It would be extraordinarily unwise if the claims for materialism or for the unity of science were to be formulated in such fashion as to require that for each distinguishable psychological state there must be one and only one corresponding brain state.

I see no way to accommodate such considerations that does not involve a wholesale employment of the notion of functional equivalence. For the point on which Sellars' argument turns is precisely that there may very well be sets of neurologically distinct brain states, whose members are nevertheless psychologically indistinguishable. In such cases, identification of the psychological state with any member of such a set produces problems with the substitutivity of identity.

It seems clear that a materialist can avoid these difficulties only at the price of assuming that the objects appropriate for identification with psychological states are sets of *functionally equivalent* neurological states. In particular, it must be true of any two members of such a set that an organism may alternate between them without thereby undergoing psychological change.

This is tantamount to saying that a materialist must recognize as scientifically relevant a taxonomy of neurological states according to their psychological functions. Such a taxonomy defines a "natural kind" (although very likely not the same natural kind as emerges from purely anatomical and biochemical considerations). Thus, a reasonable version of materialism might hold that psychological theories and neurological theories both involve taxonomies defined over the same objects (brain states), but according to different principles. What we require of the members of a set of anatomically similar brain states is *not* what we require of the members of a set of functionally equivalent brain states. Yet in neither case need the classification be arbitrary. The psychological consequences of being in one or another brain state are either distinguishable or they are not. If they are distinguishable, it is a question of fact whether or not the distinction is of the kind that psychological theories recognize as systematic and significant.

It is tempting to suppose that there must be only one principle of sorting (taxonomy by physical similarity), on pain of there otherwise being chaos, that either there is *one* kind of scientifically relevant similarity or there is *every* kind. It is, however, unnecessary to succumb to any such temptation. What justifies a taxonomy, what makes a kind "natural," is the power and generality of the theories that we are enabled to formulate when we taxonomize in that way. Classifying together all the entities that are made up of the same kinds of parts is one way of taxonomizing fruitfully, but if we can find other principles for sorting brain states, principles that permit simple and powerful accounts of the etiology of behavior, then that is itself an adequate justification for sorting according to those principles.

It would seem, then, that both the traditional approach to materialism and the traditional approach to the unity of science are in need of liberalization. In the first case, if he is to accommodate the sort of problem that Sellars has raised, the materialist will have to settle for identifications of psychological states with sets of functionally equivalent brain states, and this means that the materialist thesis is at best no clearer than the notoriously unclear notion of functional equivalence. In the second case, it appears that if the doctrine of the unity of science is to be preserved, it will have to require something less (or other) than reducibility as the relation between constructs in neurology and those in psychology. It seems, then, that scientific theories can fit together in more than one way, perhaps in many ways. If this is correct, then reduction is only one kind of example of a relation between scientific theories that satisfies reasonable constraints on the unity of science. It would be interesting to know what other kinds of examples there are.

FOUR

The Logic of Simulation

References to computers, real and hypothetical, have recently achieved a certain prominence in philosophical discussions of psychological explanation and of the mind-body problem. On the one hand, the claim that computers can (or can be imagined to) behave in the ways in which organisms do suggests a new way of formulating the goals of theory construction in psychology. For it may be argued that understanding the operations of a computer capable of simulating a given form of behavior is tantamount to understanding the behavior itself. While this suggestion is notably in need of qualification, it can by no means be rejected out of hand. Simulating behavior is related in important ways to explaining it, and a philosophical account of psychological explanation ought to clarify that relation.

Second, the possibility of successful computer simulations of behavior recalls Descartes' problem about the propriety of applying terms that are used to designate the mental states of organisms to machines that behave in the ways in which organisms do. A computer in a cartoon prints out "*Cogito ergo sum.*" Assuming that the argument is valid, could it be sound? A version of the mind-body problem that asks whether the fact that a machine can simulate intelligent behavior could ever be grounds for saying that the machine is intelligent has at least the value of raising the traditional difficulties about the relation of mental to behavioral language in a new form. Moreover, it forces us to consider how closely and in what ways our willingness to use mental terms is tied to our willingness to consider whatever such terms apply to "to be a person."

In the present chapter we shall discuss both of the questions just referred to. But it is worth noticing at the start that one could avoid the second question entirely, and the first in some part, simply by declining to talk about "machine behavior." For, of course, from the fact that a machine can simulate behavior it does not necessarily follow that the machine can therefore behave—no more does it follow from the fact that I can simulate your check signing by forging your name that I can therefore sign your checks.

If to refuse to apply behavioral language to anything but organisms is merely to make a decision about linguistic policy, then surely that decision is impeccable: one may talk in any way one pleases. If, however, this is to amount to *more* than a decision about linguistic policy, it will need to be argued for. For the intuitive inappropriateness of talking about machine behavior is not *equally* apparent for every kind of machine: there are clearly machines that we would be more easily persuaded to speak of as behaving than we would, say, of phonographs and automobiles. We cannot, therefore, arrive at a reasoned decision about the propriety of references to machine behavior until we have at least identified whatever factors distinguish those kinds of machines that tempt us to use behavioral language from machines of other kinds and have provided reasons for discounting such factors.

Conditions Upon Simulation

If we are to examine the relation between explanation and successful simulation, we shall have to set conditions for achieving the latter. I propose to say that a machine successfully simulates the behavior of an organism when trained judges are unable to discriminate the behavior of the machine from the behavior of the organism in relevant test situations. It should be remarked, to be sure, that this way of talking begs some difficult questions. For I have provided no explication of the notion "relevant test situation," and it is easy to see that what tests are relevant depends in important ways upon the type of behavior that is being simulated.

In evaluating a putative machine simulation of behavior, as in other kinds of experimentation, it is impossible (and *a fortiori* unnecessary) to control all the variables at once. And though there are indefinitely many variables that would presumably *never* be relevant to determining whether simulation is successful (and that must, therefore, always be controlled), there are presumably indefinitely many others whose relevance to determining the success of the simulation is a function of the type of behavior under study.

Thus, for example, while the judge must never be allowed to discriminate the behavior of the machine from that of the organism by investigating their respective physiologies, it by no means follows that any discrimination he can make on the basis of their comparative behaviors alone is ipso facto relevant to determining the success of a simulation. Comparison of the acuity of their sensory mechanisms might be more or less irrelevant to determining the success with which a computer plays chess while precisely that comparison could conceivably be critical in evaluating a computer simulation of, say, the operations that are involved in detecting lines and edges.

Related considerations suggest grounds for being suspicious of any attempt to provide an a priori enumeration of the necessary conditions upon simulating a form of behavior. Thus, it is self-evident that an adequate simulation of a form of behavior must reproduce whatever theoretically relevant relations that kind of behavior bears to other things that the organism does; if, for example, the frequency of dreaming is related to the restfulness of sleep, or if the content of dreams is related to the unconscious wishes of the dreamer, then an adequate simulation of dreaming must also exhibit these relations. But this sort of consideration argues against the possibility of providing an a priori account of the necessary conditions upon successful simulation in any very informative way. Forms of behavior may be interconnected as subtly as one pleases; in such cases as the ones just mentioned, the very existence of such interconnections emerges only as the result of sustained psychological research. Psychological research is thus, continuously if implicitly, redefining the necessary conditions upon the successful simulation of the types of behavior it examines. To attempt to enumerate such conditions a priori would therefore be tantamount to attempting to anticipate the results that such research will yield.

For the same sorts of reasons, it is at best not evident that a priori attempts to state general *sufficient* conditions for successful simulation could prove fruitful.

The "Turing Game"

The best known of such attempts is due to Turing,[1] who suggested, in effect, that a machine simulation of human cognitive behavior should be considered to be successful if competent judges cannot distinguish between the machine and a person on the basis of their answers to questions of the judges' devising. In fact, however, it seems apparent that either satisfaction of this condition is not sufficient for successful simulation of thinking or else its formulation must be question begging in much the same way as the one I proposed above.

That Turing's test, strictly interpreted, does not provide a sufficient condition for successful simulation of human cognitive behavior is evident from the fact that it could be passed by machines that are incapable of indefinitely many performances that lie well within the capacities of normal humans; performances that may well be argued to constitute types of intelligent behavior. Thus, the ability of a machine to pass Turing's test would not, by any means, entail that it could also obey such simple commands as "Mind the baby while I go shopping." This is in part because the ability of a machine to win at Turing's game would not ensure that the machine is able to integrate the results of its putative mentations with its ongoing behavior in anything like the normal human fashion.

One could imagine various kinds of cases in which these sorts of incompetence might be exhibited by a device that was capable of doing well at the Turing game. Consider the following scenario (I assume the standard Turing situation: the experimenter cannot see the machine and the machine is allowed to lie).

EXPERIMENTER: The pea is either under the red shell or under the green one, and it's not under the green one. Which shell is it under?
MACHINE: The red one.
EXPERIMENTER: Pick up the shell it's under.
(MACHINE *picks up the green shell.*)
EXPERIMENTER: Which one did you pick up?

MACHINE: The red one.
EXPERIMENTER: Very good.

Any one of a number of things might have gone wrong here, several of which are compatible with playing the Turing test successfully. It is possible, for example, that the machine is merely color-blind, or that it has got the reference relations for "red" and "green" wrong. But it is equally possible that the machine suffers from some more or less general inability to act as the results of its computations require that it should act. Whether one ought to say of a machine (or a person) in this state that it can think, that it is rational, or that its behavior is intelligent is, perhaps, a moot point.

Such examples suggest that there must be a great variety of cases in which a machine that is capable of passing Turing's test might nevertheless exhibit decidedly nonhuman behavioral incapacities. Turing's question-answering machine is, in fact, precisely what it seems to be: a question-answering machine, a device that simulates one of the indefinitely many behavioral capacities which jointly constitute the rationality of a normal person—the ability to provide reasonable answers to questions that are put to him in his native language. It is a very long step from doing this to satisfying sufficient conditions upon the simulation of intelligent human behavior *tout court,* and it is perhaps not a step in any very clearly defined direction. Is there, after all, any reason to suppose that it *must* be possible to enumerate some set of behavioral capacities such that whatever exhibits them ipso facto thinks like a person? [2]

Clearly Turing's suggestion that the machine be examined on its ability to answer questions was not intended to deny the relevance of the simulation of rational action to adjudicating the adequacy of a machine's simulations of ratiocination. Turing would presumably have been dissatisfied with a device that could answer questions about how to boil water if it routinely put the kettle in the icebox when told to brew the tea. Turing's test was intended only to ensure that the judges' discrimination between the machine and the organism is made in a way that is fair to the machine; that is, to ensure that all *irrelevant* distinctions between the machine and the organism are controlled for. If, however, Turing's test is put in this way, it turns out to beg precisely the important questions: *What kinds of grounds* ought to be considered fair? *What sorts of distinctions* ought to be considered relevant?

It must be emphasized that should it prove impossible to enumerate the necessary and/or sufficient conditions for the successful simulation of behavior in an informative way, then the problem of controlling simulation experiments would be more, not less, like the problem of controlling physical experiments. For precisely the kinds of difficulties that we have raised about formulating the conditions for the successful simulation of behavior also arise when we try to formulate the conditions for well-controlledness of experiments outside psychology. What makes an experiment in physics well controlled is, after all, simply that we have accounted for all the variables that we have reasonable grounds for supposing to be relevant. It is not usually possible to enumerate the relevant variables a priori, for which variables are reasonably considered to be relevant is determined by the theoretical context in which the experiment takes place, just as which variables are in fact relevant is determined by which theory happens to be true.

In short, to say that it is a sufficient condition for successful simulation that the behavior of a machine should be indistinguishable from the behavior of an organism on any relevant ground is analogous to saying that it is a sufficient condition for the well-controlledness of a physical experiment that the experimental controls cannot be relevantly criticized.

Both remarks are patently necessarily true, but neither would appear to be very informative.

Simulation and Explanation

Granted the notion of a relevant control (i.e., granted that we can tell what controls are relevant in the theoretical context in which a given simulation experiment is run), it is possible to define "successful simulation" in the admittedly question-begging way suggested above. But it then becomes evident that the technical ability to simulate successfully certain aspects of, for example, human behavior, by no means entails that we are able to explain that behavior. Any phonograph of reasonable fidelity can, for example, successfully simulate human speech production in the sense of "simulate" that is currently at issue: there are situations in which a sophisticated judge could not distinguish the productions of a phonograph from those of a speaker. One can make a start at understanding the relation between simulation and explanation by attempting to understand why no one seems to have ever been seriously tempted to think of such simulations as having explanatory value.

One could easily mistake the sound of a phonograph playing in the next room for the sound of someone speaking. Yet explanations of what happens when phonographs play recordings of speech are not in any sense explanations of speech production; nor would it be reasonable to say that phonographs can speak; nor is hearing a phonograph play recordings of speech in the next room properly described as hearing something being spoken in the next room. Why?

In the first place, it might be suggested that recordings of speech are always recordings of *someone's* speech—that is, are always causally connected to some utterance by some person. Hence, they lead the sort of second-class existence that shadows, mirror images, and echoes have. The existence of recordings of utterances is dependent on the existence of utterances *tout court*. Hence, what phonographs do when they play a recording of speech must be distinguished from what people do when they speak.

The problem that this objection raises is technical, however, rather than logical. For there not only could but do exist machines that are capable of synthesizing speech *de novo*—for example, of producing a sequence of speech sounds that corresponds to some spectrographic pattern or to some set of internally generated instructions. Yet despite the fact that the speech they produce is not, or need not be, causally connected to particular utterances by particular persons, there is no inclination to call such speech synthesizers "speaking machines."

What then is wrong with phonographs? Or, to put it the other way around, what would a machine simulation of speech have to accomplish in order to be a serious candidate for an explanation of how people speak? Note that this question is distinct from the much harder question "What would a machine simulation have to do, in order to be a serious candidate for an explanation of *how people are able to speak to some purpose?*" For the ability to speak a language to some purpose is presumably logically related to the ability to understand the language, while the ability to produce phonologically and syntactically regular sentences in the language is presumably not. Phonographs, however, have *neither* of these abilities: if they do not speak, they do not babble either. They do not speak at random for they do not speak at all.

Two things are wrong with phonographs in this connection, and each is important for understanding explanation by simulation. In the first place, at the very best, phonographs do what speakers *do,* not what speakers *can do.* In the second place, phonographs do what speakers do, but they do not do it in the way in which speakers do. These points need to be investigated at length.

Suppose we played a recording of precisely the set of sentences that constituted Smith's life history of utterances. In that case, the phonograph would have produced precisely the same sequences of speech sounds as Smith has produced, yet the operations of the phonograph do not in any sense explain Smith's verbalizations, and, as previously noted, there is no inclination to call the phonograph a "talking machine." This is related to the fact that, although the phonograph has said whatever Smith has said, there are, nevertheless, relevant statements about Smith's performance that do not hold for that of the phonograph.

Clearly, the utterances that a speaker does in fact produce are a selection from among the set of utterances that he could produce, given the appropriate motivation and circumstance. There are all sorts of things that one is never called upon to say, but that one knows perfectly well how to say and would say, if the situation warranted. "My automobile has turned into a pumpkin again" is, in that sense, an available English utterance form, although it is one that most speakers probably go through their lives without ever finding the occasion to employ. The (obviously infinite) set of English utterance types thus forms a space of possible behaviors from which the actual verbalizations of a given speaker (or, for that matter, of all English speakers throughout the history of the language) constitute a more or less unsystematic sample.

It is thus evident that one of the things that is wrong with simulating Smith's utterances by phonograph is that a phonograph record, however long-playing it may be, nevertheless fails to represent Smith's utterances as a selection from the set of possible English utterances—that is, fails to represent them as a selection from among the things that Smith could have said and would have said, had the times proved propitious. Unlike Smith, the phonograph cannot be said to know the language it speaks. If only for that reason, the phonograph fails to approximate even that part of Smith's linguistic competence that accounts for his ability to babble in English.

Behavioral Performance Versus Behavioral Competence

One can, of course, generalize the above considerations to apply to nonverbal behavior. In doing so, one arrives at the notion of the behavioral repertoire (as opposed to the actual performance) of an organism as the primary object of simulation. The potential behavior of the organism defines a space of which its actual behavior provides only a sample. A necessary condition upon explanation by machine simulation is thus that the space of possible machine behaviors should be identical in theoretically relevant respects to the space of possible organic behaviors—that is, that relevant counterfactuals that are true of the behavior of the organism must also be true of the behavior of the machine.

On this view of what is required in order for a simulation to count as an explanation, the machine must at least be able to produce whatever behaviors the organism is able to produce, since the requirement that the machine simulate the behavior actually produced by the organism would seem to be at once too weak and too strong—too weak because, as we have seen, it might be satisfied for certain kinds of behavior by such uninteresting machines as phonographs; too strong because we must allow for the possibility that differences in the local circumstances of the machine and of the organism may lead them to choose to produce different behaviors, even in cases in which the behavioral repertoires from which the choices are drawn are identical.

It goes without saying that we arrive at information about the behaviors that are potentially available to an organism, primarily (perhaps only) by way of inductive inferences from the behavior organisms are observed actually to produce. (Often we arrive at information about the set of behaviors available to a machine in very much the same way since, notoriously, machines often fail to have precisely the capacities their programmers intended them to have.) Analogously, comparing the observed behavior of the machine with the observed behavior of the organism is a way of inductively certifying that the behavioral repertoire of the machine is, in relevant respects, identical with the behavioral repertoire of the organism.

Both these inferences—from the properties of observed behavior to the character of the repertoire from which it is drawn, and from similarities between the observed behavior of the machine and the observed behavior of the organism to correspondences between their behavioral repertoires— have the usual properties of inductive extrapolations. For example, it counts strongly toward establishing the identity of their repertoires that the machine and the organism should behave similarly when confronted with a situation that neither of them has previously encountered. This is a special case of the general principle that it is success in predicting new cases that counts most toward establishing the lawful status of an empirical generalization. Since such inferences raise no problems that are not already familiar from philosophical discussions of induction and theory construction in the physical sciences, we shall not consider them further here.

It is worth adding, however, that if these considerations are correct, we can see why neither the Turing proposal, nor any other could, in principle, provide a characterization of a test procedure which, when successfully carried out, satisfies a logically sufficient condition for the explanatory adequacy of an attempted simulation. What we are ultimately attempting to simulate when we build a psychological model is not the observed behavior of an organism but rather the behavioral repertoire from which the observed behavior is drawn. Our evidence for success in the former of these undertakings is, primarily, our success in the latter. Patently, however, this is *inductive* evidence: our basis for believing that the behavioral repertoire of the machine matches that of the organism is that we have achieved a match between observed subsets of these repertoires. Inductive data do not, however, entail the hypotheses they support. Hence no number of successful simulations could provide *logically* sufficient grounds for the explanatory adequacy of a psychological model.

Simulation Compared with Other Forms of Explanation

It is of primary importance to note that the considerations we have encountered in discussing the question "When does simulating behavior count as explaining it?" have exact analogies in discussions of the confirmation of conventional psychological theories and, indeed, in discussions of the confirmation of theories in sciences other than psychology.

We have said that a necessary condition of the explanatory adequacy of a simulation is that it prove to be capable of accounting for the known data. That is to say, the behavior that the organism is observed to produce must be included in the behavioral repertoire of the machine, if the machine's program is to count as an adequate psychological theory of the organism. But we have also required that the simulation support relevant counterfactuals. The repertoires of the machine and of the organism must be identical in respect of those behaviors that we have *not* observed as well as in respect of those we have.

Both these sorts of requirements are, however, completely general in their application to scientific theories. A theory that predicts the observational data but fails to predict correctly the relevant counterfactuals is a false theory, whatever the area of science in which it may be entertained. Indeed, the fact that the one but not the other succeeds with the counterfactuals determines a fundamental distinction between a law of nature and a mere empirical generalization, and it is surely a necessary condition upon the adequacy of a scientific theory in psychology or elsewhere that it correctly distinguish laws from generalizations.

I am in effect suggesting that the question "What is the relation between simulating behavior and explaining it?" is a special case of a general question about scientific theories— namely, "What is the relation between being compatible with the experimental data and being true?" It would obviously be a mistake to claim, in the special case, that simulation bears *no* relation to explanation, just as it would equally and obviously be a mistake to claim, in the general case, that correspondence with the data bears no relation to truth. Nevertheless, one does not want to say that correspondence with the data provides a *sufficient* condition in either case. Although the issues are complicated, it seems sufficiently clear that to adopt a way of evaluating theories that requires only that they be compatible with the observations would be to ignore important conditions of adequacy that scientific theories are and ought to be required to satisfy: that they prove successful with counterfactuals, that they provide a basis for distinguishing between laws and regularities, and that they project their inductions in the simplest way that is consonant with accommodating the data.

It has been widely noted that these requirements are closely interconnected. For truth claims for counterfactuals are characteristically substantiated by appeals to laws of nature, and the lawful character of an inductive generalization is certified, in part, by showing that it satisfies reasonable simplicity constraints. Thus, to require of a scientific theory that it be adequately simple, that it deal satisfactorily with counterfactuals, and that it distinguish laws from generalizations, is possibly to state only one condition, although a condition that can be expressed in several different ways.

These considerations hold equally in the case of explanation by simulation. To suppose that the explanatory adequacy of a simulation would be entailed by its ability to accommodate the observational data is simply to underdetermine the constraints upon the confirmation of theories of this kind. In particular, it would be to provide no way of choosing between the indefinitely many nonequivalent models that, in principle, may always be constructed in such a way as to yield predictions compatible with any given set of observational data. This kind of choice must be made precisely by appeal to those considerations of simplicity by which the status of putative laws and counterfactuals is also determined.

Simulation and Functional Equivalence

It is, then, a very important condition upon the explanatory adequacy of a machine simulation of the behavior of an organism that the observed behaviors of the machine and those of the organism be drawn from behavioral repertoires that are identical in all theoretically relevant respects. But even this does not provide a logically sufficient condition for explanatory adequacy. For a machine that can do (precisely or approximately) what Smith can do, even if it is inclined to do it (only or approximately) when Smith is, might nevertheless do it in ways that are very different from the way in which Smith does it. Now, I think it is simply analytic that a correct psychological explanation of Smith's behavior is one that correctly describes the psychological processes upon which his behavior is contingent. Hence, for an adequate simulation to be an adequate explanation it must be the case *both* that the behaviors available to the machine correspond to the behaviors available to the organism *and* that the processes whereby the machine produces behavior simulate the processes whereby the organism does.

Suppose we had a theorem-proving machine that proved theorems of the propositional calculus by using the method of truth-tables. Then the potential output of this machine (viz., the infinite set of theorems of the propositional calculus) would be, in one relevant respect, identical to the potential output of anyone who knows how to do proofs in propositional calculus. Yet the machine would be inadequate as an explanation of theorem-proving insofar as it does not do proofs in the same way as a human mathematician does them. In particular, since it is incapable of employing the sorts of heuristics that mathematicians can employ, the operation of the machine provides very little (possibly no) insight into the mental operations that constitute this kind of mathematical reasoning.

What this sort of case shows is that quite general correspondences between machine and organic behaviors may often turn out to be, in an important sense, artifactual. In cases like this, and presumably in most cases that affect the psychologist's practice, the differences between the computations that underlie machine and organic behavior become evident if we extend appropriately the demands upon the simulation. In particular, the machine and the mathematician, since they employ different proof procedures, will not generally find the same theorems easy to prove; what it takes a relatively long time for the machine to prove, the mathematician may prove relatively quickly. Hence, if the machine is required to simulate not only the mathematician's ability to prove theorems, but also his complexity judgments and other relevant aspects of his theorem-proving, it should sooner or later become evident that simulation by the use of truthtables is inadequate. Here, as elsewhere, the psychological theorist attempts to determine the identity of machine processes with organic psychological processes by broadening the demands upon simulation so as to include ever more subtle parameters of the organism's behavior. Extending the area within which identity is required between the repertoire of the organism and that of the machine is thus itself a strategy for satisfying the demand that the internal processes of the machine be relevantly similar to those of the organism it simulates.

There is no guarantee, of course, that this strategy will work. Differences between the processes that underlie machine and organic behavior might, in principle, elude even the most ingenious experimental inquiries. This is one of the forms that "inductive risk" takes in the case of explanation by simulation. The psychologist must acknowledge the logical possibility that he has opted for the wrong machine, even after he has tried in every way he can think of to distinguish between the behavior of the machine and that of the organism. In just the same way, the physicist must acknowledge that any amount of experimental success is logically compatible with the possibility that he has opted for the wrong theory. Neither psychological nor physical explanation is thereby placed in doubt.

Let us say that a machine is *weakly* equivalent to an organism in some respect when the behavioral repertoire of the machine is identical with the behavioral repertoire of the organism in that same respect. We can then say that a machine is *strongly* equivalent to an organism in some respect when it is weakly equivalent in that same respect *and* the processes upon which the behavior of the machine is contingent are of the same type as the processes upon which the behavior of the organism are contingent.[3] We might then seriously suggest that to simulate behavior by a machine that is strongly equivalent to an organism in respect to that behavior is ipso facto to explain the behavior. But this formula, of course, also begs all sorts of questions.

For one thing, the distinction between weak and strong equivalence is vacuous whenever identity of a form of behavior is determined by reference to the operations that underlie its production. For example, which form of behavior is instanced (what sentence is uttered) by an utterance of the phonemic sequence "John likes old men and women"? Clearly, the answer to this question must depend upon the way in which that behavior was integrated by the speaker— that is, upon whether "old men" formed a segment of the utterance. But that, in turn, depends upon the sequence of mental operations that underlie its production—upon the particular grammatical rules employed in integrating it.

To understand the implications of this sort of example, consider a device that purports to be weakly equivalent to some speaker in that it claims to be capable of enumerating precisely the set of sentences that the speaker will accept as grammatical. In order for the putative weak equivalence to hold, it must be the case that the behavioral repertoire of the machine includes a sequence that corresponds to "John likes old men and women." The present question, however, is whether it must include *two* such sequences, one corresponding to the bracketing (old men) (and) (women) and one corresponding to the bracketing (old) (men and women).

The existence of this sort of behavioral ambiguity suggests that the notion of weak equivalence between an organism and a machine can be made clear only relative to some antecedently specified notion of a *level of description*. This is not surprising, since weak equivalence requires that each type of behavior available to the organism must also be available to the machine, and the individuation of types is possible only where a vocabulary for the description of tokens has been fixed.

Thus, in the example just mentioned, a device that is weakly equivalent to a speaker *at the phonological level* need specify "John likes old men and women" only once. A device that claims weak equivalence at the more abstract level of constituent analysis must specify it twice. The two devices thus differ in regard to how many forms of behavior an utterance of the sentence may instance.

To summarize: a claim of weak equivalence between an organism and a machine entails a claim that the repertoire of the machine includes all the forms of behavior that are available to the organism. The truth of such a claim therefore depends critically on the choice of a theoretical vocabulary in which the relevant behaviors are to be described. If the production of a sentence, for example, is represented as the production of a sequence of sounds, the demand for weak equivalence between a man and a sentence-producing machine is a quite different requirement from the one we get when the sentence is represented as the production of a sequence of words or of phrases as well as a sequence of sounds. This is immediately evident from the existence of behavioral ambiguities—cases in which more than one form of behavior may be instanced by a given overt gesture. For wherever there are behavioral ambiguities, there must exist two or more levels of description, on one or more of which the gesture has a univocal representation and on one or more of which it does not. Claims for weak equivalence may therefore be true at the former levels, but not at the latter.

It must be emphasized that the choice of the level(s) of description in terms of which the notion of weak equivalence is explicated is by no means at the arbitrary disposal of the psychological theorist. Not every choice of levels yields a systematic representation of the organism's behavioral repertoire, and the question of whether a putative level is artifactual may, therefore, involve some of the deepest issues in theoretical psychology (*vide* the current dispute in linguistics over the existence of the "phonemic level"—i.e., over whether morphemes are sequences of discrete phonemic entities or sequences of bundles of properties—wherein phonology recapitulates ontology).

Clarification of the complex of relations between the notion of weak equivalence, the specification of the levels of behavioral description, and the analysis of the type/token relations for behavior—all these are prerequisites for a serious philosophical analysis of the structure of psychological theories. Fortunately, however, they are not prerequisite to a preliminary understanding of the goals of such theories. For the latter purpose, it is possible to dispense with the notion of weak equivalence altogether. In order to do this, we need only accept the convention that we individuate forms of behavior by reference not solely to the observable gestures output by an organism but also to the sequence of mental operations that underlie those gestures. That is, we count two overt gestures as instances of different forms of behavior whenever they are the consequences of different mental operations. Then the requirement that the machine and the organism be *strongly* equivalent in some respect is simply the requirement that their behavioral repertoires be identical in that respect.

A much more serious problem with the suggestion that explanation is simulation by a strongly equivalent machine is the following: strong equivalence requires that the operations that underlie the production of machine behavior be of the same type as the operations that underlie the production of organic behavior. But we have provided no criteria for determining when machine operations and organic operations should be regarded as relevantly similar.

The problem is the usual one: two operations being of the same type must surely be compatible with physical dissimilarities between the devices that perform them. One might put it that the predicates "realize the same sequence of operations" and "operate according to similar mechanical principles" are simply not coextensive. If you classify together all machines with the same program, you will have a mechanically heterogeneous set of machines; if, on the other hand, you classify together all mechanically similar machines, you will have a set of machines whose input-output relations may be arbitrarily heterogeneous. Classifying machines by reference to the information-handling operations they perform is one way of classifying them; classifying machines by the types of mechanical transactions they exhibit in the performance of those operations is another, and quite different, way of classifying them. There is no mystery about this unless one is committed to the view that *all* taxonomies must ultimately reduce to classification by physical similarity.

What is true of these relations among machines is also true of the relations between machines and organisms. No one supposes that organic processes must be simulated by machines that are themselves composed of flesh and blood, if the simulation is to count as explanation. But what then are the requirements upon the relation between the internal operations of the organism and those of the machine that simulates it?

If, in short, there is no mystery, there is nevertheless a problem. For the criteria for saying that two machines are mechanically similar are fairly clear. But what shall we say of the conditions upon similarity of data processes? One way of putting the problem is to say that the requirement of strong equivalence between machine and organism is neither more nor less clear than the notion of functional equivalence for it is in terms of functional equivalence that strong equivalence must be defined. In particular, it is a logically necessary and sufficient condition for strong equivalence between an organism and a machine that is weakly equivalent to it (1) that, for each psychological process that is involved in the production of organic behavior, there should be a corresponding data process involved in the production of machine behavior, and (2) that the corresponding processes should be functionally equivalent. The clarification of the program of explaining behavior by simulation thus rests upon the clarification of these two conditions. Though much more needs to be said, the following remarks may be of some use in this connection.

Since condition (1) requires isomorphism between the processes underlying machine and organic behavior, it requires *a fortiori* that we have some way of counting psychological processes. Condition (2) requires functional equivalence between each process that underlies machine behavior and the corresponding process underlying organic behavior— that is, it requires at least that each machine state be related to the machine's behavior in the same way as the corresponding organic state is related to the behavior of the organism. Hence condition (2) requires *a fortiori* that we must have some notion of the ways in which psychological processes *can* be related to behavior.

We thus find ourselves once again at the point at which the clarification of a key concept in psychological metatheory can reasonably look for aid from the development of sophisticated "object level" psychological explanations. For evidently the question "What counts as one psychological process?" is logically connected to the question "What processes are distinguished by the vocabularies of empirically successful psychological theories?" Further, the question "When are two psychological processes related to behavior in the same ways?" is logically connected to the question "What kinds of relations between behavior and psychological processes are distinguished by empirically successful psychological theories?" Attempts to individuate theoretical entities a priori or to determine a priori what sorts of lawful relations they might bear to observables make no more sense in psychology than they would in physics.

I take this to be a fairly serious point. The functional character of a machine state is determined by its total role in the machine's computational processes as well as by its relation to machine behavior in the narrow sense of machine output. To determine functional equivalence between individual machine states and corresponding organic states thus requires a more or less general correspondence between the psychology of the organism and that of the machine. Nothing can be functionally equivalent to, say, a pain if it fails to bear the same relation to motives, drives, and so on that pains do. Therefore, no machine can exhibit states that are functionally equivalent to pain states if it does not also exhibit states that are functionally equivalent to drives and motives.

The extent and nature of such interconnections among psychological states is precisely what psychological theories attempt to make explicit. The present point is that, in doing so, they implicitly determine the substantive conditions upon functional equivalence for the states and processes that they postulate. Nor is it easy to see how such determinations could be made *prior* to successful theory construction in psychology.

It should also be noted that, in whatever way we decide

to construe the notion of functional equivalence, it *must* be so understood as to permit of grading. It makes sense to say that two processes are *more* or *less* alike in their relations to behavior, or that the operations of two mechanisms are *more* or *less* similar, and that fact is intrinsic to the nature of attributions of functional equivalence.

In a gross account of the operations of an internal combustion engine, one might count carburetors and fuel injectors as functionally equivalent on the grounds that both serve to aerate the fuel and to get it into the cylinders. But, of course, refined accounts distinguish in all sorts of ways among their operations, as well as among the consequences of their operations, and an explanation of the way in which injected engines produce power in a Mercedes-Benz 300 SL would be only approximately correct as an explanation of the way in which carbureted engines produce power in an XKE Jaguar.

Therefore, if the notion of explanation by simulation rests upon the notion of relevant functional equivalence between machine operations and organic operations, it follows that simulations can be more or less satisfactory or revealing or explanatory, depending not only on the extent of the overlap between the behavioral repertoire of the organism and that of the machine but also on the fineness of grain demanded of the functional correspondence between the machine processes and the organic processes.

Finally, it may be remarked that the clarification of the notion of functional equivalence is demanded not only for the solution of present problems in psychological metatheory but also in order to mark important relations within psychology proper.

However one construes the relation between neurological and psychological constructs, it can hardly be denied that a proper, not to say traditional, goal of investigations in physiological psychology is the determination of the functional organization of the nervous system. But, as we remarked in Chapter III, there is no a priori basis for supposing that a parsing of the nervous system according to the psychological function that its parts perform would correspond in any simple way to parsings that are effected in terms of its gross topographical, morphological, or biochemical divisions. (Even the a posteriori evidence for such correspondences is, on the whole, less striking than one might have expected. Lashley's doctrine of "equipotentiality" would, if I understand it correctly, amount *inter alia* to a denial that such correspondences generally hold.) In short, the notion of a functional parsing of the nervous system demands the definition of some notion of functional equivalence for sets of neurological states that may in principle be arbitrarily different in their physical characteristics. But if such a relation is in fact defined for such sets of states, it is ipso facto defined for sets that include the corresponding states of machines, since a machine state is functionally equivalent to functionally equivalent neurological states, if it has in common with each of them whatever they are required to have in common with one another. If, in short, we understand what it is for neurological states to be indistinguishable in psychologically relevant respects—for example, to be identical in their behavioral consequences, then we ipso facto understand what it would be for some state of a machine to be functionally equivalent to such neurological states (e.g., to be related to machine behavior in the way in which the neurological states are related to organic behavior).

Simulation and the Mind-Machine Problem

Thus far we have been concerned with the question: "When, if ever, would simulating organic behavior by machine count as explaining it?" I have suggested that this question may properly be regarded as a special case of the question: "Under what circumstances does the ability of a theory to account for the relevant observational data make that theory true?" In either case, the answer requires that the counterfactuals predicted by the theory be true and that the theoretical states, entities, and processes posited by the theory exist. On this view, a machine program is simply a way of realizing a psychological theory, and it explains the behavior it simulates only insofar as it satisfies the usual methodological and empirical constraints upon such theories.

I said at the outset of this discussion that problems about explanation by simulation go hand in hand with certain ways of construing the mind-machine problem. What, then, does the discussion so far imply about whether it would ever make sense to say that machines think?

Suppose that we have a machine that satisfies whatever experimental tests we can devise for correspondences between its repertoire and that of some organism. Suppose, too, that there is some process P that is essentially involved in this simulation—that is, if the simulation did not involve P, it would either fail to account for the data or else would fail to satisfy reasonable simplicity conditions. It may now be asked whether this state of affairs would ipso facto justify the attribution of processes that are functionally equivalent to P to the organism whose behavior we have simulated.

It would appear, from the considerations discussed above, that nothing depends on putting this question in terms of machine simulation. We might just as well have asked: "Suppose we have a psychological theory that posits P and which we have good reason to regard as true. Would we therefore be justified in attributing P to the organism whose behavior the theory is alleged to explain?"

It seems to me that this is the point at which philosophical questions about psychology merge with more general philosophical questions about scientific theories. For, as far as I can see, the only reasons that would hold for refusing to attribute *P* to an organism under such conditions would equally be reasons for supposing that *all* theoretical entities are fictions or mere logical constructs. That is, they would be reasons for believing that the fact that a theoretical term appears in a well-confirmed scientific theory is never grounds for existential assertions about its putative denotatum, or that all such assertions, however well warranted, are somehow always *façons de parler*. I think that such views are certainly wrong, but this is not the place to debate them.

We have seen that if it makes sense to say that machines behave at all, then there should be corresponding sense to saying that the processes that underlie machine behavior could, in principle, be functionally equivalent to those processes that underlie organic behavior. Nor is it prima facie evident that a process that is functionally equivalent to thinking ought not to be *called* thinking. So perhaps the question ought to be "Would it ever make sense to say that machines —that is, machines of the right kind, machines that simulate intelligent behavior in the strong sense of simulation that is tantamount to explanation—*don't* think?"

And to this question the answer is "Of course." We can make any distinctions we choose to make, and a perfectly good reason for refusing to apply mental predicates, or behavioral predicates, to machines is that they *are* machines. True enough, to refuse to talk of machine thought or machine behavior would be to decide on a linguistic policy; the present point is that it would not necessarily be to decide on an *irrational* policy.

There is nothing about the internal operations of a piano that cannot be accounted for by the principles of mechanics. In the technical sense of "machine," a piano is a machine— but *only* in the technical sense. In nontechnical talk, we do not call a piano a machine, for the good and sufficient reason that it is an instrument, and, in ordinary English, the categories *instrument* and *machine* are mutually exclusive. *Ought* we to call pianos machines? We could; and for certain purposes, it would be convenient to do so. It would obviate the necessity, for example, of explaining that pianos are technically machines, during the course of our explanations of how pianos work. The point however is that explaining how they work is only one (and not the characteristic one) of the ways in which we have to deal with pianos. There is no obvious reason why we should decide to let that purpose determine the way in which we talk about pianos. On the contrary, all things considered, there is every reason why we should talk in a way that takes note of the similarities between pianos and electric guitars, rather than talking in a way that takes note of the similarities between pianos and drawbridges. The purposes that we characteristically entertain toward pianos are, after all, very like those we characteristically entertain toward electric guitars, while they resemble hardly at all those that we characteristically entertain toward drawbridges. (This has to do with the fact that it is easier to imagine a piano repairman conceptualizing a piano as a machine than to imagine a concert pianist doing so.)

If we had a machine that behaved like a person, and if it did so for the right reasons, then we could use mental predicates in talking about that machine. That is, there would be nothing to stop us from doing so: it would not be an obviously irrational practice, and it is tedious to insist that indulging that practice would be indulging an equivocation upon the mental predicates. Indeed, the analogies between what the machine does and what a person does, as well as between the explanation of what the machine does and the explanation of what a person does, might well strike us as so persuasive that we would find it "natural," "right," or even "inevitable" to apply to the machine terms that we had earlier reserved for persons. That is to say, just as distinctions sometimes strike us as worth preserving, so they sometimes strike us as worth ignoring. Sometimes, or for some purposes, we overlook differences that we know to be there.

On the other hand, there is nothing in logic that would *require* us to overlook such differences. Whether we ought to decide to exploit them is thus only in a very broad sense a question about the rationality of our decision. In particular, it need not be a question for a priori settlement since neither of the alternatives need lead to conceptual incoherences. It is possible, as Putnam has remarked, to imagine a state of affairs in which the appropriate thing to say of someone who refused to use certain mental predicates with regard to machines is not that he is irrational but that he is inhumane.

There is thus a question of empirical fact and a question of linguistic policy; what is important is to distinguish between them.

It is a question of fact, and not of how we should decide to talk about the facts, whether, or to what extent, a given kind of organic behavior is the consequence of psychological processes that are functionally equivalent to some machine processes. Such questions are settled in the way in which questions about the existence and character of theoretical entities are usually settled—namely, by demonstrating the explanatory adequacy of the theory that postulates those entities. In the present case, we demonstrate functional equivalence between machine and organic processes by determining that the psychological theory realized by the machine's program provides an adequate and simple account of the organism's behavior. We have seen no reason to believe that such determinations are problematical in any way that is not common to the confirmation of other kinds of scientific theories.

The question of policy is whether, given a machine process that is known to be functionally equivalent to some organic psychological process, we ought to *call* the former by the term we use to refer to the latter. This is perhaps not much of an issue, but of such issue as there is, one is inclined to say "There is no 'ought' about it." Clearly, the empirical considerations that determine that there exists a functional equivalence between organic and machine states do not also determine how we should talk about such equivalences. So if, as I have suggested above, there is no matter of logical principle at stake here, it would seem that there is no matter of empirical fact at stake either.

There is a persistent suggestion in the philosophical literature that once we have noted the analogies between the overt behavior of a machine and that of an organism (or, for that matter, between the overt behavior of an animal and that of a person), we have taken into account all the questions of fact that could be relevant to deciding whether an application of mental language to the machine is warranted. It is suggested that our decisions about such ascriptions amount simply to decisions that the behavioral analogies do or do not justify talking about the machine (the animal) in the same way as one would talk about a person.

This sort of approach appears to be implicit in some characteristically enigmatic passages in Wittgenstein's *Philosophical Investigations*—for example: "We do not say that *possibly* a dog talks to itself. Is this because we are so minutely acquainted with its soul? Well, one might say this: If one sees the behavior of a living thing, one sees its soul." [4] It might seem to follow that a machine or an animal that exhibits the behavioral capacities that are characteristic of a person is ipso facto entitled to the mental properties ascribed to persons. That conclusion is, however, by no means entailed. To attempt to draw it would be to overlook a point of the kind that Wittgenstein sometimes calls "grammatical."

"But a machine surely cannot think!—Is this an empirical statement? No. We only say of a human being and what is like one that it thinks. We also say it of dolls and no doubt of ghosts too." [5] Presumably, on Wittgenstein's view, if we *were* to ascribe thoughts to machines, that would be because we had allowed the behavioral analogies to persuade us to think of machines as "like human beings," in somewhat the same way as the physiognomic analogies sometimes persuade us in the case of dolls. In such fashion, the facts about behavior might finally tempt us to alter our linguistic policies.

We can now see that this sort of view is right in stressing the role of decisions of linguistic policy in decisions to use mental language about machines. But it is wrong in supposing that the only factual questions in view concern the analogy or disanalogy between machine and organic *behaviors*. The important factual question is whether the computational processes that underlie machine behavior are functionally equivalent to the psychological processes that underlie organic behavior—whether, in short, the psychological theory that is realized by the machine's program is true of the organism. That is, the empirical facts to which decisions of linguistic policy must be sensitive are not primarily analogies between overt machine behavior and overt organic behavior, but rather correspondences between the psychology of the machine and that of the organism. If this fairly obvious point has been widely overlooked, it is perhaps because the philosophical discussion has been haunted by the assumption that questions of literal truth and falsehood cannot be raised about theoretical entities; that, in psychology and elsewhere, facts about the data are really all the facts there are.

I suspect, however, that the question to which these remarks have been addressed is not really the question that people worry about. For what one wants to know is not whether some machine processes might be functional equivalents of some organic psychological processes. Nor is it whether it could ever be rational or linguistically correct to *say* that a machine feels pains, or thinks, or has gotten confused, or whatever. Rather it is whether, in very fact, the machine hurts, or cogitates, or finds itself bewildered. Failure to distinguish between linguistic correctness and truth has often been the beginning of bad philosophy, and perhaps this question is, after all, left over when the linguistic proprieties have been attended to. If it is, it's too hard for me.

NOTES

Introduction

1. Cf., for example, Meehl and Cronbach (1956).
2. Cf. Quine (1961), Putnam (1960), Kuhn (1962), and Hanson (1961). I have tried, in this volume, to benefit from the pluralistic account of science that such works articulate.
3. For a very useful collection of papers in this area, see Canfield (1966).

CHAPTER ONE *Is Psychology Possible?*

1. Hamlyn (1957), p. 20
2. Grice (1961).
3. It is difficult to exaggerate the service that Grice has performed by reviving and insisting upon what amounts to the distinction between semantic and pragmatic implication. Take an example almost at random. It is sometimes argued that to say of an act that it was voluntary is somehow to imply that it was "special" (e.g., one says of a dangerous mission that it was undertaken voluntarily, but one does not say of Smith that he voluntarily brushes his teeth). The moral is supposed to be that there is something wrong with the problem of free will. For to say *either* that our behavior is, in general, voluntary, or that it is, in general, not, is taken implicitly to violate the supposed rule that "voluntary implies special."

   I think everyone suspects that there is something wrong with this argument. Somehow, one wants to say, the claim that brushing one's teeth is a voluntary act, although possibly odd, is not incoherent; it does not have the feel of a self-contradiction. One understands what has led some philosophers to assert it and others to deny it in just the way that one doesn't understand what could lead someone to assert that circles have corners. The point of Grice's suggestion that such implications as "voluntary, so special" might best be treated as pragmatic is that it allows us to understand *both* why it sounds odd to say that Smith brushes his teeth voluntarily *and* why one might hold that that statement, even though odd, is true.

4. Kuhn (1957), p. 40.
5. See, for example, Peters (1958).
6. Ryle (1949), p. 225.
7. Wittgenstein (1953) argues in a similar style in paragraph 154: "Try not to think of understanding as a 'mental process' at all—for *that* is the expression which confuses you. But ask yourself: In what sort of case, in what kind of circumstances, do we say, 'Now I know how to go on' . . ."
8. Ryle, *op. cit.*, p. 225.
9. *Ibid.*
10. This example is due to Paul Ziff in conversation.
11. Ryle, *op. cit.*, p. 227.
12. *Ibid.*, p. 226.
13. *Ibid.*, p. 229.
14. *Ibid.*, p. 231.
15. The problem of machine recognition of tunes has not, to the best of my knowledge, been widely studied. But the comparable problems of machine recognition of speech and script have engaged the attention of computer experts for a number of years. It is therefore some indication of the complexity of the perceptual processes involved that it is not at present technically or theoretically possible to build a machine that produces phonemic transcriptions of utterances (viz., that recognizes speech), or a device that can recognize letters in arbitrarily different (but legible) styles of type. All normal children can, of course, master both these tasks by the age of six.
16. Cf. Liberman (1957).
17. Melden (1961), p. 88.
18. Davidson (1963).
19. For more discussion than this fairly obvious point probably warrants, cf. Putnam (1962a), Hanson (1961), and Fodor (1964a).
20. Peters (1958), p. 12.
21. *Ibid.*, p. 13.
22. To maintain that psychological explanations may be causal

is not, of course, to maintain that *all* explanations of behavior are causal explanations, or that all ordinary-language psychological terms designate causes. There is, for example, a sense of "explain" in which it is a synonym of "justify"; correspondingly, there are cases in which to explain behavior is to provide not its cause but its rationale. The detailed analysis that would be required to distinguish these cases and to determine which ordinary-language psychological terms go with which sort of explanation is, however, well beyond the scope of this chapter.

CHAPTER TWO   *Behaviorism and Mentalism*

1. For a defense of behaviorism that is vitiated by its failure to provide a motivated a priori specification of what may count as a description of behavior, cf. Ziff (1962).
2. Ryle (1949), *passim*.
3. Wittgenstein (1953), *passim*. See also Chihara and Fodor (1965).
4. Strawson (1959).
5. That the confusion of mentalism with dualism has not been restricted to philosophy and psychology has recently been made clear. For a discussion of the role this error played in the thinking of Bloomfield and of American structural linguists in general, cf. Katz (1964).
6. It is indeed one of the more important differences between the logical character of radical behaviorism and the logical character of radical materialism that while both maintain the identity of each mental state with some nonmental states, the propositions that enunciate the radical behaviorist's reductions of mental to behavioral predicates are supposed to be analytic. Hence this reduction amounts to a true eliminative definition. By way of contrast, the materialist's identifications of mental with physical states are presumably enunciated by contingent propositions and hence provide no basis for the elimination of mental language from psychological theories. Just as chemistry is incomplete unless it contains at least one contingent proposition in which "water" occurs (i.e., "Water is H_2O"), so, on the materialist's view, a completed psychology would occasionally need to use mentalistic language, if only in formulating the relevant truths of psychophysical identity.
7. For a really outstanding example of what might be called the fallacy of misplaced necessity see Cavell (1958) where

it is maintained that our comments about our speech habits, when true, are truths of transcendental logic. For discussion, see Fodor and Katz (1963).
8. This circularity in the pedagogical argument for behaviorism was first pointed out in Jarvis (1964).

CHAPTER THREE *Materialism*

1. Cf. Oppenheim and Putnam (1958).
2. Cf. Putnam (1960a), Chihara and Fodor (1965).
3. R. Abelson has suggested to me a way out of the apparent paradox—namely, that we call an entity "theoretical" only when existence claims about *all* entities of that kind are based upon inferential evidence, that is, that no member of a class of entities is theoretical if any member of that class has been observed. This allows us to say either that Martian trees are theoretical entities (i.e., because they are *Martian* trees and no tree growing on Mars has yet been observed) or that Martian trees are *not* theoretical entities because they are Martian *trees* and observations of trees (albeit of trees growing on Earth) are not rare. In short, there are two concepts that are in need of simultaneous adjustment: the concept of a theoretical entity and the concept of two entities being of the same kind. If slack develops in one place, it can be taken up in the other.
4. Cf. Hempel (1950).
5. For discussion of this point, cf. Fodor (1964a).
6. For further discussion, cf. Fodor (1964a).
7. Cf. Putnam (1960a).
8. Cf. Oppenheim and Putnam (1958), p. 6.
9. Meehl (1965), where the argument is attributed to Sellars.

CHAPTER FOUR *The Logic of Simulation*

1. Turing (1950).
2. Cf. Gunderson (1964) for a discussion of this sort of point. It should be added, however, that Turing himself appears to be half-inclined to think of his test as providing a sort of stipulative characterization of the truth conditions upon assertions that a machine is able to think. This he, of course, has every right to do.
3. The notions of weak and strong equivalence used here were suggested by the ones that were introduced by Chomsky and

Miller (1963) in a discussion of conditions of empirical adequacy upon grammars of natural languages. The relations are, however, loose and analogical.

4. Wittgenstein (1953), p. 113.

5. *Ibid.*

REFERENCES

Canfield, J. (1966). *Purpose in Nature.* Englewood Cliffs, N.J.: Prentice-Hall.

Cavell, S. (1958). "Must We Mean What We Say?" *Inquiry,* I (1958), 172–212.

Chihara, C., and J. Fodor (1965). "Operationalism and Ordinary Language," *American Philosophical Quarterly,* II (1965), 281–295.

Chomsky, N., and G. Miller (1963). "Introduction to the Formal Analysis of Natural Languages," in R. Luce and E. Galanter (eds.), *Handbook of Mathematical Psychology.* New York: Wiley. Vol. II, pp. 269–700.

Davidson, D. (1963). "Actions, Reasons, and Causes," *Journal of Philosophy,* LX (1963), 685–700.

Fodor, J. (1964). "On Knowing What We Would Say," *Philosophical Review,* LXXIII (1964), 198–212. (a)

———— (1964). "A Review of L. Jonathan Cohen's 'The Diversity of Meaning,'" *Journal of Philosophy,* LXI (1964), 334–343. (b)

————, and T. Bever (1965). "The Psychological Reality of Linguistic Segments," *Journal of Verbal Learning and Verbal Behavior,* IV (1965), 414–420.

————, and R. Freed (1963). "Some Types of Ambiguous Tokens," *Analysis,* XXIV (1963), 19–23.

————, and J. Katz (1963). "The Availability of What We Say," *Philosophical Review,* LXXII (1963), 57–71.

Garrett, M., T. Bever, and J. Fodor (1966). "The Active Use of Grammar in Speech Perception," *Journal of Perception and Psychophysics,* I (1966), 30–32.

Grice, H. P. (1961). "The Causal Theory of Perception," *Proceedings of the Aristotelian Society,* Suppl. Vol. XXXV (1961), 121–152.

Gunderson, K. (1964). "The Imitation Game," in A. Anderson

(ed.), *Minds and Machines*. Englewood Cliffs, N.J.: Prentice-Hall. Pp. 60–71.

Hamlyn, D. (1957). *The Psychology of Perception*. London: Routledge & Kegan Paul.

Hanson, N. (1961). *Patterns of Discovery*. Cambridge: Cambridge University Press.

Helmholtz, H. (1856). J. P. C. Southall (ed.), *Helmholtz's Treatise on Physiological Optics*. New York: Dover.

Hempel, C. (1950). "The Empiricist Criterion of Meaning," in A. J. Ayer (ed.), *Logical Positivism*. New York: Free Press. Pp. 108–129.

Jarvis, J. (1964). "Private Languages," *American Philosophical Quarterly*, I (1964), 20–31.

Katz, J. (1964). "Mentalism in Linguistics," *Language*, XL (1964), 124–137.

Kuhn, T. (1957). *The Copernican Revolution*. Cambridge: Harvard University Press.

———— (1962). *The Structure of Scientific Revolutions*. Chicago: University of Chicago Press.

Liberman, A. (1957). "Some Results of Research on Speech Perception," in S. Saporta (ed.), *Psycholinguistics*. New York: Holt, Rinehart and Winston. Pp. 142–152.

Meehl, P. E. (1965). "The Compleat Autocerebroscopist: A Thought-Experiment on Professor Feigl's Mind-Body Identity Thesis," in P. Feyerabend and G. Maxwell (eds.), *Mind, Matter and Method: Essays in Philosophy and Science in Honor of Herbert Feigl*. Minneapolis: University of Minnesota Press. Pp. 103–180

————, and L. Cronbach (1956). "Construct Validity in Psychological Tests," in H. Feigl and M. Scriven (eds.), *Foundations of Science and the Concepts of Psychology and Psychoanalysis*. Minnesota Studies in the Philosophy of Science. Minneapolis: University of Minnesota Press. Vol. II, pp. 174–204.

Melden, A. (1961). *Free Action*. London: Routledge & Kegan Paul.

Oppenheim, P., and H. Putnam (1958). "Unity of Science as a Working Hypothesis," in H. Feigl, G. Maxwell, and M. Scriven (eds.), *Concepts, Theories and the Mind-Body Problem*. Minnesota Studies in the Philosophy of Science. Minneapolis: University of Minnesota Press. Vol. II, pp. 3–36.

Peters, R. (1958). *The Concept of Motivation*. London: Routledge & Kegan Paul.

Place, U. (1956). "Is Consciousness a Brain Process?" in V. C.

Chappell (ed.), *The Philosophy of Mind.* Englewood Cliffs, N.J.: Prentice-Hall. Pp. 101–109.

Putnam, H. (1960). "Minds and Machines," in S. Hook (ed.), *Dimensions of Mind.* New York: New York University Press. Pp. 138–164. (a)

———— (1960). "Dreaming and Depth Grammar," in R. J. Butler (ed.), *Analytic Philosophy.* New York: Barnes & Noble. Pp. 211–235. (b)

Quine, W. V. (1961). "Two Dogmas of Empiricism," in *From a Logical Point of View.* 2nd ed. Cambridge: Harvard University Press.

Ryle, G. (1949). *The Concept of Mind.* London: Hutchinson.

Strawson, P. F. (1959). *Individuals.* London: Methuen.

Turing, A. (1950). "Computing Machinery and Intelligence," *Mind,* LIX (1950), 433–460.

Wittgenstein, Ludwig (1953). *Philosophical Investigations.* New York: Macmillan.

Ziff, P. (1962). "About Behaviorism," in V. C. Chappell (ed.), *The Philosophy of Mind.* Englewood Cliffs, N.J.: Prentice-Hall. Pp. 147–150.

Index